THE NORTHWEST PASSAGE

THE NORTHWEST PASSAGE

From the *Mathew* to the *Manhattan:*
1497 to 1969

Bern Keating

*with exclusive color photography
by Dan Guravich*

Rand McNally & Company
Chicago   New York   San Francisco

Book Cover and Title Page Artwork: *Woman Who Lives in the Sun*, 1960, Stone cut by Kenojuak, Cape Dorset; and the print on page 24 reproduced with permission of La Fédération des Coopératives du Nouveau-Québec.

Reproduced with permission of the West Baffin Eskimo Cooperative, Cape Dorset, N.W.T., are prints on pages 11, 12, 23, 51, 69, 70, 137, 138.

The print on page 52 is reproduced through the courtesy of the Holman Eskimo Cooperative, Holman Island, N.W.T.

The black-and-white illustrations are reproduced through the courtesy of Derek Balmer, Bristol (England) Art Gallery, portrait of John Cabot, page 92; Sir Albert Hastings Markham, *A Whaling Cruise to Baffin's Bay and the Gulf of Boothia* (London: Low, Marston, Low, and Searle, 1875—Chicago Public Library), 100; National Maritime Museum, Greenwich, England, 98; Newberry Library (Chicago), Franklin, Bylot, and Belcher Memorial, 126; Newberry Library, Edward E. Ayer Collection, 96, the *Hecla*, *Griper*, and crews, 120; Norman Poole, the *Mathew*, 92; G. Barnett Smith, *Sir John Franklin and the Romance of the North-West Passage* (New York: Fleming H. Revell Company, ca. 1900), portrait of Sir John Franklin, 126.

The color illustrations on pages 90, 93, 118-119, are by courtesy of *The Humble Way*, Humble Oil & Refining Company, and those on pages 116, 123, are by courtesy of *The Lamp*, Standard Oil Company (New Jersey).

Book Design by Irv Basevitz

CONTENTS

Other Books by Bern Keating:

The Mosquito Fleet
A Young American Looks at France
A Young American Looks at Italy
A Young American Looks at Denmark
The Horse That Won the Civil War
The Life and Death of the Aztec Nation
Zebulon Pike
The Invaders of Rome
Chaka, King of the Zulus
The Grand Banks *in collaboration with Dan Guravich*
Alaska

THE NORTHWEST PASSAGE

For Lionel and Lu
Dear friends and gentle hearts

PREFACE

By the mid-thirteenth century the highborn jarls of medieval Norway had known peace for two generations; they lived the valiant deeds of their Viking forefathers only through sagas sung by wandering skalds, epic poems celebrating perilous days of sea roving, discovery, and conquest when the Norse peoples were young. For a prince of the court, an unknown bard sang *The Mirror of the King*, telling of cruel hardships braved by Viking sea wolves in the western marches of the kingdom, in the ice-choked channels around Iceland and Greenland.

A century and more earlier the jarls had abandoned the Viking freebooter's hard life on northern waters, and their sons had lost the taste for long journeys through icy seas seeking unknown lands in the supremely seaworthy but mercilessly exposed dragon boats. So the unknown singer had to answer for his bewildered patrons the eternal question of the comfort-loving homebody: Why will a sane man leave his warm hearth to suffer the terrors of unknown Arctic waters?

The bard's insight into the seafaring man who spurns snug harbors for uncharted fields of polar ice holds true today, 700 years after he first sang his heroic song:

> If you want to know what men look for in that land or why men go where there is such danger to their lives, it is the threefold nature of men that lures them on. One part of man wants fame, for man goes where there is great danger to make himself famous. Another part of man wants knowledge, wants to see those places he has heard of and find out if they are as he has been told. The third part is the desire for riches, for man pursues wealth wherever he thinks he can find it, even though he must pass through great dangers.

Chapter 1

"THRILLING REGION OF THICK-RIBBED ICE"

Owl Attacking Snow Goose by Kiakshuk

Man Pulling A Walrus by Parr

Fingers stiffened by sub-zero cold, our sailors from the S.S. *Manhattan* clumsily lifted rocks from the cairn on Beechey Island, "the post office of the Arctic," and dropped into it a can containing our historic document, to prove we had passed that way. It was an elaborately worded message, giving the date, our numbers and mission, and a few lofty sentiments suitable to a historic occasion. But essentially it was simply a cry to posterity that we too had once lived and had walked this bleak and forbidding land.

Leaning against the gale, I walked across the plateau to the edge of the cliff and peered down through tears whipped up by the bone-chilling wind and through twilight gloom—all the daylight the Arctic sky allowed at that late season. Far below, four headstones dotted the frozen strand. Three headstones mark the graves of the first sailors to die among the crew of the disastrous Franklin expedition, the most famous crew ever to attempt the sea-lanes across the frozen top of North America, the fabled Northwest Passage. The fourth marks the grave of a young mariner who died aboard a rescue ship sent to find the lost Franklin sailors.

By the standards of their day in 1846, those three of Franklin's men are the lucky ones; they rest quietly in decent burial. The bones of their 127 shipmates, the cream of the Royal Navy's youngest and strongest officers and seamen, were scattered across 500 miles of frozen wasteland. They lay where they dropped, unnoticed by their comrades, who staggered on in a hopeless flight southward to escape the hideous rotten-mouth scurvy death that inexorably pursued. The last ones alive found no health in eating the disease-wasted flesh of their dead comrades—a horrid meal that filled the belly but did not nourish, did not gain them a minute of life.

What made those lusty, youthful sailors leave the flowered fields and cream-skinned maidens of England for this death trap, this hostile world of ice and gloom, polar gales and numbing cold, starvation and bone-aching scurvy?

They had come in pursuit of a dream, the same dream that had brought me and my shipmates to the frozen channels through the Canadian Arctic archipelago, the dream of carving a shipping lane across the top of the world through the Northwest Passage.

Like the Vikings of old and the seagoing men of the North since then, we had all come seeking fame, knowledge, and gain.

Almost 500 years ago, even while Christopher Columbus still deluded himself that he had found a westward passage to Cathay, hardheaded sailors of the northern seas suspected that the Genoese had found only a huge landmass, a wilderness inconveniently blocking the way to the riches of the East. Despite popular belief that Columbus first revealed the spherical shape of the earth, European navigators had known that great truth for centuries: A glance at a globe showed northern navigators that the shortest route between home port in Europe and the exotic wealth of the Orient lay across the top of the world, through an undiscovered but hoped-for Northwest Passage piercing the New World barricade across the road to the Pacific.

Less than five years after Columbus returned from his first voyage, bold Welsh and West Country English sailors of Bristol, under the command of John Cabot, sailed west to probe at the newly discovered land block across the sea-lanes, looking for an opening to the western ocean. Some historians believe Cabot disappeared on the second voyage, in the icy approaches to the passage—first known victim of the quest for a short northwest route to fame, knowledge, and riches, a quest that has lasted for almost five centuries.

During those centuries hundreds of mariners died; the carcasses of their ships litter the ocean floor. Finally, during this century, two explorer's cockleshells, a few icebreakers, and a nuclear submarine have slipped through the channels. But no commercial vessel had even attempted the passage since the early, innocent days of the Age of Exploration, before the Western world learned at terrible cost how grim were the passes through the northern seas. As recently as 1958, a distinguished Canadian geophysicist called the Northwest Passage "impractical and useless." In 1966 the Dominion hydrographer for Canada told a countrywide radio audience that the only way Canadian Arctic mineral or oil resources would ever be exploited would be by cargo or tanker submarines.

But in 1968, at Prudhoe Bay on the North Slope of Alaska, Humble Oil & Refining Company and the Atlantic Richfield Company brought in a well which independent consultants say proved an oil field of at least 25 billion barrels, making it by far the largest strike in North America. With 3,200 miles of muskeg and forest between the wellhead in Arctic Alaska and the gas pump on the East Coast of the United States, costs of overland transport would be staggering. So marine experts at Humble revived the dream of moving wealth between East and West through the Northwest Passage surface sea-lanes.

They leased the S.S. *Manhattan*, at 150,000 tons the largest tanker under the American flag, and converted it to an ice-breaker-oceanographic research vessel to test the feasibility of the route through Canada's Arctic islands for ships big enough and powerful enough to smash ice that would have crushed the smaller vessels that had tried the passage before. Project directors recruited an elite crew from the Humble tanker fleet and organized a task force of marine architects and ice scientists. They invited me and my photographer partner to make the trip as chroniclers of the historic voyage.

Cost of the gamble on a single voyage soared to $36 million, and Atlantic Richfield and British Petroleum boosted the pot with bets of another $2 million each. The ante was breathtaking, even for the oil business, but the stakes were enormous:

Should the Northwest Passage prove feasible for moving crude from Alaska to the East Coast of the United States, savings of oil transport could run as high as hundreds of thousands of dollars daily for 20 years or more.

As it had for 500 years, the Northwest Passage again worked its charm, despite the long record of death and disaster visited on earlier seamen who had sought riches along that way.

The lure of the Northwest Passage can be seen only on a globe.

In the sixteenth century the Flemish cartographer Gerardus Mercator, with a flourish of topological abracadabra, drew a flattened two-dimensional version of the earth's spherical three-dimensional surface. For short voyages, Mercator projection charts were so convenient to spread on chart tables that navigators willingly overlooked gross distortions of distances that increased rapidly toward the poles. They overlooked the distortions all the more willingly if they meant to sail only in pussycat-tame waters below the sixtieth northern parallel.

Schoolteachers enthusiastically adopted the flat Mercator projection as almost the sole teaching aid for geography lessons, because the flat map hung easily before a blackboard, visible to a seated class. Mercator charts did not force a class to crowd around as they had to when using a necessarily smaller globe. Admittedly the flat Mercator maps distorted northern regions beyond any practical use, but in the temperate zones, where most schoolchildren live, distortions were within tolerable limits. So schoolmasters understandably sacrificed strict accuracy for convenience. After all, which of their students would need to know true distances between perpetually ice-locked bays in a frozen sea?

And so dozens of well-schooled generations have been reared to think as inhabitants of Flatland, only vaguely conscious that they live on a sphere. Virtually none of even the best educated has ever pondered that three out of four of us live in a narrow band between about 35° and 50° north, roughly between the latitudes of Chattanooga, Tennessee, and St. John's, Newfoundland, or in Europe between Gibraltar and London. About 80 percent of the world's industry lies in that narrow strip on the northern half of the globe.

For a mariner, then, the problem of moving the world's goods from source to market is a northern problem. Which makes the Mercator chart a useful yet treacherous aid, with its built-in distortions of northern distances.

Moving from the familiar Mercator map of the world to the globe is a jolting experience. Without the help of a globe, who would suspect that the harbor equidistant from the great ports of Vladivostok, Tokyo, New York, London, Rotterdam, Le Havre, Hamburg, and Copenhagen is the little Eskimo village of Sachs Harbour on the southwest corner of Banks Island, southwesternmost of the Canadian Arctic archipelago? Sea voyages between those great eastern and western seaports by conventional southern routes involve immense detours of thousands of miles.

On a Mercator projection, for instance, the sea voyage from New York to Alaska by the Panama Canal appears about the same distance as the trip through the Northwest Passage. Measurement on a globe shows it twice as long.

Obviously, as an open sea the Arctic Ocean would be the main route for the world's commerce, with more sea traffic than the North Atlantic carries today.

But there is one little hitch.

Ice covers 5.5 million square miles of the Arctic Ocean. The ages-old and granite-hard pack around the North Pole sprawls 1,400 miles south toward Alaska and on the other side 700 miles south toward Siberia. Across the top of North America, the ice problem is aggravated by a maze of channels through the Canadian Arctic islands that trap drifting polar floes driven by the westerly winds and stack them in some places more than 100 feet deep.

And we know almost nothing about that ocean and its ice, or about the nature of life in that northern world.

With the perversity of man, far more scientists study the face of the moon, or even of Mars and Jupiter, than concern themselves with the immense world of ice, one that is within a two-hour jet flight of most scientific centers.

Aboard the S.S. *Manhattan*, at the invitation of Humble officials, the elite of the non-Communist world's glaciologists accepted the unique chance to pursue their studies in a laboratory deep in virgin ice fields, many of them never before visited by man. Scientists from the army's Cold Research Environmental Laboratory, the University of Alaska, the U.S. Coast Guard, the Canadian Department of Transport, and other agencies joined the task force. They did not overcrowd the ship.

Dr. Charles Swithinbank of the Scott Polar Institute at Cambridge talked to me about the minuscule population of his academic discipline.

"Since the birth of the science, there have been only one hundred glaciologists; and, of those, fourteen have been killed in polar accidents in recent years.

"A strange neglect when you consider that eighty percent of the earth's fresh water is locked up in ice. If the world's ice melted, the seas would rise almost three hundred feet and ninety percent of us would be blowing bubbles. If you spread the world's ice over the world's land surface like butter over toast, it would cover every remotest spot, even the Fiji Islands, six hundred feet deep.

"If even a fraction of the ice cover of the earth were, instead of frozen water, some newly discovered form of homogeneous rock, thousands of scientists would flock to its study. But more people study the horoscopes of cats than study ice."

Excluding the lifeless Greenland ice cap, almost half the part of the world that can be called Arctic by any criterion lies in the Canadian coastal strip north of the tree line and the Canadian Arctic archipelago, split in half by the main channels of the Northwest Passage.

The islands alone cover 517,000 square miles, almost twice the area of Texas. Spread over the immense region are perhaps 4,000 souls, slightly more than half the population of El Campo, Texas. The entire population of the Queen Elizabeth Islands north of the Northwest Passage main channels, a perpetually frozen tangle of icy straits and barren islands covering 165,500 square miles, would make a disappointing turnout for a basketball game in Itta Bena, Mississippi. The meagerness of population is not to be wondered at, for even the incredibly hardy Eskimo more than 500 years ago had to abandon the Queen Elizabeth Islands, except as a migration route to easier lands like, say, the northwestern tip of Greenland. (But those sea rovers of the Viking golden age, in their pursuit of fame, knowledge, and riches, came to the Queen Elizabeth Islands and left behind eider-duck traps of typically Norse construction to prove it.)

The Canadian Arctic is not the coldest spot on earth. Even the North Pole falls far short of registering record cold. The Antarctic suffers far lower temperatures and worse gales. Even in the Northern Hemisphere, thermometers in interior Siberia and the Yukon and Tanana valleys of the Yukon Territory and Alaska drop 20 degrees lower than along the Northwest Passage. With Alaska, three other American states—North Dakota, Wyoming, and Montana—register lower temperatures every winter than occur along the Northwest Passage. But minus 50 degrees is cold enough to form a special world. And the meagerness of precipitation in the Canadian Arctic makes life even more difficult, makes the region a frozen desert, for less moisture falls on some islands as either rain or snow than falls on Yuma, Arizona, or Las Vegas, Nevada. On Barter Island, near the Alaska-Canada border, precipitation runs as meager as in Death Valley, California, driest spot in the United States. And just inches under the soil the permafrost never melts, forming an impervious shield to probing roots, so no trees can take hold even if they were hardy enough to stand cold and drouth.

Various authorities define the Arctic as: the regions north of the tree line; the regions north of a mean summer temperature of 50 degrees; and the regions of permafrost. Since those three zones coincide almost exactly, the argument is academic. The fact is, the landscape of the Canadian Arctic archipelago is bleak, treeless, perpetually frozen just a finger length or two below the surface. Summers are brief and cool, winters long and cruelly cold for forms of life not exquisitely adapted over the ages to existence in a climate lethal to all southern species.

And yet life has somehow thrust its way into that forbidding region and maintained itself for ages.

The Canadian explorer Vilhjalmur Stefansson, in many ways the most daring and competent Arctic rambler who ever lived, said of the Arctic that it "is lifeless, except for millions of caribou and foxes, tens of thousands of wolves and musk oxen, thousands of polar bears, millions of birds and billions of insects."

But mariners are not concerned with the abundance of game, except as curiosities to brighten a dull day's passage. They are concerned with open seaways. And open water lanes are scarce in the Northwest Passage.

In winter, ice blocks all channels. In summer the western half of the Canadian island channels are choked almost as tight as in winter with cobalt-blue, granite-hard ice blown down from the ancient polar pack and jumbled by polar gales into keel-busting ridges.

Eskimos have more than a hundred words to define subtly the different kinds of ice they must contend with. But they have lived with ice for countless generations. The first Europeans of historical times who sailed into Arctic seas ventured forth with sublime ignorance. They scarcely knew floating sea ice existed, much less its complex nature and danger to seafarers. Their followers for centuries broke the backs of their little ships on barriers of ice of a thickness, hardness, and menace impossible to believe before encountering them.

The wonder is that even after the mariners of the world learned through terrible experience how dangerous was the ice of the Northwest Passage, they continued to brave it for centuries, some of the sailors volunteering, incredibly, for third and fourth voyages into regions where they had watched their shipmates rot away and die from scurvy—if they escaped starving, freezing, or drowning.

Man's stubborn assault on that formidable ice barrier is one of his proudest efforts. His failures in that grim region make poignant and heroic tragedies. His few triumphs are marvels of human doggedness and skill.

I am proud to have been a shipmate of the latest sailors pursuing that centuries-old dream.

Chapter 2
THE AGE OF INNOCENCE

Angry Bears by Pauta

Birds by Josie Paperk

Among the silly half-truths and falsehoods my generation learned in our shockingly superficial or downright dishonest history courses was the asinine notion that prior to the discovery of the Western Hemisphere in 1492 the people of the world believed the earth to be flat—except for one genius, a Genoese sailor named Christopher Columbus who persuaded a Spanish queen he could prove the world was "round" by sailing west.

Two thousand years earlier, about the same time the citizens of Rome threw out the Tarquin kings and established a republic —roughly during the time of the Battle of Marathon and the suicidal stand of the Spartans at Thermopylae—Greek thinkers had established the earth's spherical shape. About the time Hannibal crossed the Alps into Italy, long before the birth of Christ, a Greek of Alexandria named Eratosthenes had calculated the circumference of the earth to be approximately 25,000 miles. It has taken more than 2,000 years to correct his figure by a very small percentage. That same mathematician, 1,700 years before Columbus, proposed sailing west from Gibraltar to the East Indies.

Three centuries later, Greeks of the decadent period messed up the accurate geography they had inherited from their betters and recalculated the circumference of the world as 15,000 miles, a wildly inaccurate figure that did great harm during the early period of the great explorations that closed the Middle Ages. But even those mathematical incompetents never doubted the earth's spherical shape.

Perhaps some landlubbers locked deep in Europe's interior thought the earth flat, but saltwater fishermen daily saw the church steeples of home port sink below the horizon as they sailed away, and knew the earth had bulged upward between them and home. Deepwater sailors who had seen thousands of approaching vessels loom above the horizon—mast first, followed slowly by the hull—could not escape knowledge of the earth's shape. Some of the brutes laboring aloft to take in sail in winter gales may have had their minds on more immediate problems, but even the simplest navigation requires an active, inquiring mind; the pilots of western Europe had no doubt of the earth's shape.

PYTHEAS

The first explorer of northern waters who left a written record of his voyage was far more than a shrewd salt. He was Pytheas, a Greek astronomer of the booming mercantile city of Massilia, as Marseilles was called in the fourth century before Christ. That contemporary of Aristotle and Alexander the Great not only understood the shape of the earth, but calculated the latitude of his native city so accurately that many modern astronomers accept his figures without qualification and ascribe any small apparent inaccuracy to the fact that the whole city has moved somewhat to the north since Pytheas's day.

Sailors had long since noticed that one star stayed put at a constant angle of elevation in the northern sky and the heavens revolved around it. Any mathematician, even one of far less than Pytheas's stature, could figure out that only the rotation of a globe carrying the observer through a daily 360° tour of the skies could explain that phenomenon. Pytheas contributed to this already well-known fact the discovery that the true pivot point in the sky was not the polestar, but a spot of empty sky nearby; and that a navigator could get his exact latitude by measuring the angular height of that pivot spot any time, instead of waiting till exactly noon for a sun shot.

In the spring of 325 B.C. Pytheas left Massilia, in a 200-ton galley rowed by a double bank of oars, on a voyage to the north not to be equaled for a thousand years. Unfortunately, his account of the voyage disappeared even before the end of the Greek Classical period, and we know of him only through fragmentary quotations at third hand by Polybius and Strabo and other historians who lived many years afterward. Like many other stay-at-home provincials, they scoffed at wonders related by the adventurer who had wandered outside the home parish. Unhappily for their reputations, most of the very marvels they hooted at in Pytheas's account have since proved accurate to the finest detail.

Unwittingly, therefore, the mean-spirited skeptics preserved for an admiring posterity the very reputation they meant to destroy, a poetic triumph that has delighted travelers of later years who have learned to keep their adventures hidden from smirking neighbors on their return to the old hometown.

The fragments remaining of Pytheas's story tell us only a few facts. Pytheas slipped somehow through a blockade of warships from Carthage, commercial rival of Massilia, that sealed off the Atlantic at Gibraltar. He escaped into the open sea and turned north along the coast of what is now Portugal and Spain. Coming from the tideless Mediterranean, he was astonished by the twice-daily rise and fall of the sea. He demonstrated his genius as an astronomer by instantly perceiving the moon's influence.

He sailed clear around Britain, visited the Shetland Islands, perhaps picked up a Scots pilot there, and sailed north to investigate reports of a land called Thule where one day a year the sun did not set. And that land was inhabited, according to the reports of Scots sailors.

Scholars have labored mightily to identify Thule; most of them have settled on Iceland, though Fridtjof Nansen, the brilliant Norwegian student and explorer of the north, could not resist the nationalistic urge to find Thule on the far northern coasts of his homeland. In any case, Pytheas sailed north from Thule till he came to a sea covered by a substance which "can neither be traversed on foot nor by boat."

Library-bound pedants have wrestled to identify that substance. Few have ventured north to the edge of the polar pack, where there is a pulpy mass of broken brash ice and half-frozen slush that will not support the weight of a man but offers a sluggish barrier to a sailing vessel. Like the medieval scholars who cited classical authorities for the number of teeth in a horse's mouth without bothering to lift the nearest horse's lip and count, those pedants prefer to find truth through semantical exercises rather than to take a trip north into the "congealed" sea that stopped Pytheas's progress toward the pole.

Pytheas returned home to the ridicule of his immediate posterity. But his place in history is now secure as the first educated western man to cross the Arctic Circle into the polar seas.

Considering the sailing equipment available and the absence of background information to draw on, the age of Arctic exploration may have opened with its most brilliant mariner, and the history of northern navigation since may be a mild anticlimax.

THE LEGENDARY IRISH

Legends persist from the Middle Ages of venturesome Irish monks who during the sixth century sailed north and west in leather-skin *currachs*, which were strikingly similar to the Eskimo's walrus-skin *umiak*.

I can testify to the seaworthiness of such craft, for the Eskimos of Little Diomede Island in Bering Strait carried me in a *umiak* through a winter storm to deliver me aboard the supply ship *North Star* in 1968. A gale from the pole had lashed the straits into a froth and we had to run hip-deep into the surf to push the *umiak* into seas pounding the rocky shore. Although a veteran of far worse storms, some that engulfed ships within voice radio call of my ship and drowned all hands, I nevertheless was scared when I piled over the side into the *umiak* and put out to sea with only a quarter-inch of hide between me and the freezing currents below. The prospect of being marooned on the island for the entire winter, with only tattered textbooks from the native school as reading matter, was all that spurred me into that skin boat.

The *umiak* pitched sharply upward at the crest of each comber; spray formed an ice crust on our clothing. But those brown-skinned vikings of Arctic Alaska dug paddles over both gunwales and drove us out of the shoreside surf into the heaving, ice-flecked seas beyond. The ride to the *North Star* jarred the bones and made the head giddy with mad plunging, but we did not ship enough water to fill a good-sized boot.

So I believe the Irish saints could have made the Atlantic crossing in their *currachs* had they put their minds to it. And since the day a German amateur braved the ridicule of the learned to discover the ruins of Troy, wary savants have hesitated to entirely discount persistent folk tales. Too often the legends have more than a kernel of truth.

For instance, first arrivals to the New World in the great Age of Exploration reported that the Micmac Indians of Nova Scotia made the Sign of the Cross and displayed a crucifix. When first discovered, the Indians of Newfoundland had many tall, green-eyed warriors. Admittedly thin evidence for an earlier Irish presence, but still—there it is.

VIKINGS

Although the Greeks of the Classical period made some brilliant deductions about the shape and size of the earth, they let their logical minds lead them to an absurd conclusion about the earth's climate. Reasoning from the fact that a band around the center of the Northern Hemisphere had a temperate climate and that the regions grew colder to the north and hotter to the south, the Greeks extrapolated the logical notion of a globe divided into five zones—an equatorial zone too scorching to support life, neatly balanced temperate zones in the center of both hemispheres, and two polar zones of lethal cold. They even postulated the existence of a civilization comparable to theirs in the southern temperate zone, but held that distant culture forever inaccessible to dwellers of northern temperate zone cultures because of the burning equatorial zone that lay between them.

It does not surprise the worldly scholar that sound Greek astronomical works, like their astonishingly accurate calculation of the circumference of the earth, would fall into neglect while mankind continued to cling to picturesque absurdities unsupported by experience. For centuries, the doctrine of the earth's five zones stifled any urge to venture from the safe northern temperate belt.

But far to the north dwelt a rude people, most of whom could not read or write their own language, much less the exquisitely elaborate works of Greek philosophers. So they lived in liberating ignorance of the false Greek theory.

In the ninth century, the Vikings of the Danish peninsula and of the forest and fjords across the water in Sweden and Norway burst out of their northern mists and descended on the ruins of the Roman Empire. They seized half of Ireland and large chunks of England and Scotland, most of the islands north of the British Isles, parts of the French coast, and even, eventually, Sicily and southern Italy. Russia first came into existence as a state under the overlordship of Swedish warrior-traders plying their long boats up the rivers feeding into the Baltic and the White seas.

But looting the vast treasure-house of the south did not absorb all the energies of the Vikings. In their Irish domains they heard of Thule, an island to the north inhabited by Irish holy men. So, at the end of the ninth century, they sailed their snakeheaded *drakkars* into the northern seas and conquered Iceland, driving out or enslaving the Irish monks and their attendants. The swirling mists and long shadows of a feeble subarctic sun felt homier to the Northmen than the genial lands of the south, and so colonization of Iceland drained off much of their restless energy.

Soon, however, even the new lands became overcrowded, and internal quarrels forced still another move to the west into unknown seas.

Eric the Red, exiled from Iceland for having killed a neighbor in a fit of pique, talked 1,500 Icelanders into leaving with him in 24 *drakkars* to found a new home in the west. The dangerous seas around Greenland apparently caused little fright among the imperturbable Vikings, for Eric's expedition toward unknown lands was the largest cold-regions expedition in history till the U.S. Navy's Operation High Jump in 1946.

Hundreds of his colonists dropped out or drowned in shipwreck, but the survivors found a home on the southwest coast of Greenland and prospered. Within Eric's own lifetime, his neighbors and sons pushed on westward to discover the New

World, probably on the coast of Baffin Island. The Vikings ranged southward to Newfoundland and beyond, nobody knows how far.

Because they called one of the newly found coasts Vinland, historians have struggled to place them far enough south for the climate to support native grapes. But Vinland can also mean "meadowland" in ancient Norse, so much of the scholarly energy spent in pushing the Viking voyages beyond, say, Cape Cod, is wasted. The Nova Scotian coast has beautiful, broad salt meadows. In a Viking grave in Greenland, archaeologists have found lumps of coal that may have come from Rhode Island. But the only New World ruins south of the Arctic Circle positively identified as Viking are at L'Anse aux Meadows in Newfoundland at the closest possible point to Greenland across the Labrador Sea.

North of the Arctic Circle, however, Viking ruins abound. At almost 73° north on the west Greenland coast, Viking hunters left a record of their visit written in runes. Viking tools have been found north of there. Tradition says they hunted as far north as 78°, from where it is only a 20-mile hop to Ellesmere Island, the most northerly point of the Canadian Arctic archipelago.

In the grim Queen Elizabeth Islands, bordering the northern bank of the Northwest Passage, explorers have found signs of at least a semipermanent presence of Norsemen.

At home in Scandinavia and abroad in the rest of the northland, Vikings caught eider ducks—not for meat or eggs but only to pluck their down. To kill an eider or destroy a nest brought shame on a Viking. Instead, Viking hunters built shelters to attract nesting birds by setting three flat stones on edge for three sides of a square and capping them with a roof stone.

In 1875 a Scandinavian explorer reported finding one of these bird shelters on a bleak island at almost 80° north, farther north than the northernmost Eskimos have lived in centuries.

". . . [W]e came upon a bird shelter, such as the natives of Danish Greenland still use to encourage geese and ducks to settle on their shores. It consisted of four stones piled together like a miniature 'Druid's Altar', so as to form a chamber large enough to shelter a nest. Generations of eider duck had been hatched in it in security since the last wild hunter left the shore. When we found it, it held a deep nest of eider down with three eggs. . . ."

Another Scandinavian explorer at the turn of the century found the same kind of duck shelters on St. Helena Island at 76° north. He and his Scandinavian second-in-command agreed they were Norse and not Eskimo.

The interiors of most of the Canadian Arctic islands have not yet been explored. A continued oil and minerals exploration boom will almost certainly turn up more evidence of Viking penetration of forbidding regions which we are only now working up our nerve to reenter.

Hardy as they were, the Greenland Vikings nevertheless suffered a mysterious catastrophe that exterminated them. Historians have offered many explanations—starvation, lack of vitamins and consequent lowered fertility, the Black Death (the colonies disappear from record just about the time of a great plague), massacre by Eskimos. But the presence of blue eyes, light skin, and reddish hair among the native islanders (who prefer to be called Greenlanders rather than Eskimos) argue that the Eskimos probably made love, not war. The Norse apparently melted into the aboriginal culture through intermarriage.

When the next wave of exploration came, almost immediately after Columbus's rediscovery of the New World, the Greenland colony had vanished.

Portuguese sailors in the fifteenth century crossed the equator and probed the African west coast, exploding the theory of the five climatic zones by demonstrating that man could live and thrive where the old Greek theory supposed he would burn to a crisp.

Columbus was a long way from being the first navigator to suggest reaching China by sailing west. But he may indeed have been the first to suspect, from the breakdown of the theory of the Torrid Zone's inhospitality to life, that the supposed impenetrability of polar seas had been equally exaggerated. About ten years before he sailed for the west, Columbus spent time in Africa and in Iceland—possibly considerably farther north than Iceland, though debating the northern limit of his voyages can throw a roomful of historians into a bloodletting donnybrook.

At any rate, he wrote a book, now lost, denying the existence of polar and equatorial zones too cold or too hot to sustain life. In 1500 he wrote a letter to a possible patron, suggesting a trip across the North Pole. Perhaps he had started to suspect his discovery was not Cathay, but a land block across the westward route. If so, he was among the first to propose a passage from west to east by going north through polar seas.

But not quite the first.

John Cabot had already tried twice to find an opening through the New World blockage and probably had perished in the ice near the Arctic Circle. He made his first attempt in 1497, in the *Mathew*. Portuguese sailors had tried the passage between Greenland and Labrador and had turned back, defeated by the ice. The Portuguese brothers Cortereal, possibly the true discoverers of Newfoundland, had disappeared in the icy north.

Most of the early explorers of North America's coastline—including the Verrazano who gave his name to the bridge across the New York Narrows—had next to no interest in the wilderness of the New World, but were looking for a hole through the annoying land wall between Atlantic and Pacific.

Discovery of the James, Roanoke, and Hudson rivers stirred hopes, soon dashed, that they connected with the western sea. It took years to learn that the promising waterways and portages up the St. Lawrence River into the Great Lakes and down the Mississippi River led only to the Gulf of Mexico, in a great horseshoe bend that put the explorer back in the same ocean he had started from.

As explorers eliminated routes through temperate waters, the search for a passage to the east shifted northward into the ice.

FROBISHER

A frenzy of geographic speculation swept the intellectual world of the sixteenth century. Two charts were circulated widely and shaped the thinking of northern mariners about the Northwest Passage. Unfortunately, they both contained grave errors that misled seamen for decades.

In Venice, an Antonio Zeno published a chart based on an Arctic voyage that an ancestor of the same name had supposedly made in the fourteenth century. It showed Greenland and Iceland in reasonably accurate location, but it also showed a large island called Friezland between Iceland and Greenland, an Atlantic island called Icaria, and sections of the North American continental polar regions called Estotiland and Rogeo, all imaginary. Zeno's map was taken seriously, even by so eminent a mapmaker as Mercator, the Flemish geographer.

Mercator published a chart in 1569 reflecting the widely held theory that sea ice formed from shorelines outward and could not exist in the open sea. His polar regions show open, navigable water about the Pole. Unfortunately, he also reproduced most of the errors of Zeno's map.

The inexplicable vitality of falsehoods and hoaxes, like the Greek theory of climatic zones and Zeno's map, was thrust on my attention at Christmas when my daughter, knowing my interest in the Arctic, gave me an antique Dutch map of the polar region, purporting to be from the hand of the great seventeenth-century Arctic explorer Willem Barents and showing Zeno's mythical island of Friezland and the nonexistent coast of Estotiland. The chart was drawn by a superb navigator in 1598, centuries after the purported Zeno voyage, but it still carries the misleading inventions of the Zeno hoax.

In England during the early Elizabethan era a 40-year-old mariner named Martin Frobisher, veteran of an African trade almost certainly involving transport of human chattel, barely escaped being hanged, gutted, and dismembered as a pirate. Seeking an occupation subject to less risk of such disastrous loss of face, the hard-bitten sailor of little education but great ambition fell on the idea of discovering the Northwest Passage.

Like many men in any epoch, he had looked about his world and decided regretfully that he had been born almost too late, that civilization and science had reached their peak and few heroic deeds or great discoveries remained for the adventurous spirit. But Mercator's chart, and the constant buzzing in nautical circles about a short northern route from England to the Orient, awakened hope that one last task remained for the bold of heart before the world settled down forever to a humdrum life.

He called discovery of the Northwest Passage "the only thing in the world that was left undone whereby a notable mind might be made famous and fortunate."

Frobisher persuaded a group of merchants to back a trip to the northwest and got Queen Elizabeth's permission.

In June 1576, his flotilla sailed from London down the Thames. As he passed the queen's palace, he fired a salute from his cannon and Elizabeth waved her gloved hand, wishing him luck.

He was going to need it. Modern veterans of Arctic navigation are appalled at the innocence of sailors who braved those northern seas in three clumsy vessels powered only by sail. One of them, a pinnace that was scarcely more than a rowboat, had a crew of three.

Before even reaching Greenland, the flotilla fought a nine-day tempest that swamped the hopelessly inadequate pinnace, drowning the crew. The largest ship, the 25-ton *Michael*, "mistrusting the matter, privily made its way home." Frobisher's crew on the *Gabriel*, seeing their mates drowned or fleeing homeward, squalled out their distaste for continuing farther into such inhospitable waters.

Although his mainmast was sprung and fore-topmast blown away, the hard-nosed Frobisher faced down his mutinous crew and drove them back to work with the tart comment that "the sea at length needs must have an endynge." Which it did, and before the *Gabriel* had its own threatened "endynge."

Then Zeno's map began its evil work. Frobisher searched the seas for Zeno's imaginary island of Friezland and the coast of Estotiland. Beginning with that part of his journey where he expected to but did not find Friezland, Frobisher was lost and so were the home geographers who later appraised his work.

He sailed between icebergs so high that he said clouds played about their tops. Frobisher impressed the stay-at-homes with the lofty altitude of his cloud-piercing icebergs, but I have sailed the same waters when the clouds played about my shoelaces, for those waters spawn more fogs and low-scudding clouds than any others in the world. Frobisher showed his boldness and seamanship by heaving to in the lee of great icebergs for protection from high seas, a technique adopted by most sailors who followed him into those iceberg lanes.

On July 13, a storm tilted the *Gabriel* on its side. The open-waisted vessel shipped tons of water and sank almost to the gunwale bar, lolling helplessly on the waves without steerageway.

The crew's hopes collapsed and they gave up the fight, but the captain, tightroping along the gunwale, cut adrift the tangled cordage and the broken mizzenmast to free the vessel from their soggy hamper. The lightened ship rose and spewed water from the scuppers. For two days they ran with bare masts before the storm. But they survived.

On July 29, the captain spied a cape he called Elizabeth Foreland. He had no real idea where he was, but modern geographers have identified his foreland as Resolution Island at the mouth of Hudson Strait, later to be a departure point of many tragic and futile searches for the Northwest Passage in Hudson Bay.

At that time of year, the ice—covering 480,000 square miles of the inland seas beyond, an area as big as Texas, plus Mississippi, Arkansas, Louisiana, and Oklahoma—rushes through the bottleneck of Hudson Strait into the open sea.

Discouraged by the clashing, grinding, heaving masses of ice, Frobisher sailed up the coast and found a long channel leading westward with an exciting current running seaward—all the proof the optimistic Frobisher needed that this passage connected with a western sea.

At the mouth of the channel, Frobisher found a small village of Eskimos living in sealskin tents. After complex and cautious negotiations conducted in sign language, he persuaded an Eskimo to come aboard the *Gabriel* and engaged him as a pilot for the channel. He sent the Eskimo to his village in a boat manned by five of his sailors. His boat and oarsmen rounded a point and vanished from his sight forever.

Frobisher waited five days for their return, fired cannon and sounded trumpets, but received no response.

(The story of the fate of that boat crew persisted among the Baffin Island Eskimos for generations. Apparently, the boat crew enthusiastically took the chance to escape from the dangerous and backbreaking occupation of sailing under Martin Frobisher, considering life among savages on a hostile coast preferable to the *Gabriel's* forecastle. Several years after their desertion, they became homesick and built a small shallop for a desperate effort to sail to England. The Eskimos tried to dissuade them, warning that it was a bad time of year for seafaring; but they left anyhow and disappeared from history.)

A few days after the disappearance of Frobisher's men, a flotilla of *kayaks* and *umiaks* approached the *Gabriel*. Frobisher spied the very Eskimo who had gone off with the missing men in the lead canoe. Frobisher enticed him close to the ship by ringing a small bell and holding it over the side as though offering a gift. When the Eskimo reached for the bell, Frobisher grabbed his wrist and heaved the man, *kayak* and all, into the ship's waist, demonstrating that the doughty captain apparently had muscles as hard as his will.

The *Gabriel* set sail for home without probing farther into the promising fjord, and arrived in England on October 9, 1576, with only an Eskimo and his canoe to show for the voyage. And a bit of black rock picked up on the beach.

The Eskimo captive was a mild sensation in London society before he languished and died, apparently a victim of English cooking. But the bit of rock unexpectedly set off a stampede. Two chemists reported that glittering streaks in the stone were only fool's gold, but an alchemist swore it was a rich vein of the real gold. London's merchants preferred to believe the optimistic report and put up the money for a return trip to Frobisher Bay and the unknown land to the west, called by Queen Elizabeth (and still called) Meta Incognita ("destination unknown").

Next year, Frobisher sailed again, but this time with a mission to gather as much ore as his ships could carry, rather than to search for a Northwest Passage. The queen added to the original *Michael* and *Gabriel* a leviathan, comparatively speaking, of 200 tons, named the *Ayde*.

They sailed from the Orkney Islands on June 8, 1577, and on July 4 raised land. Stubbornly following the worthless Zeno map, they "knew it to be Freeseland," and were misled into rediscovering a fictitious island instead of the very real Greenland they had reached.

Misinformed he may have been, but Frobisher was a crack pilot, for he sailed along the Greenland coast four days, struck off westward, and made his landfall at the Meta Incognita with no groping.

Ashore, Frobisher tried to grapple another Eskimo to the ground, but even his giant strength could not hold his slippery quarry. While escaping to his boat, the captain caught an Eskimo arrow in his rump. One of the sailors, a Cornish wrestler, used his science on another Eskimo and brought him in alive. The captive, incidentally, reported by signs that the five deserters of the previous voyage had not been harmed.

Several gentlemen of the company asked permission to walk inland a hundred miles or so to explore the country, but Frobisher insisted the first job was to load the ships with ore. When they found a lode, Frobisher showed the urgency of the mission by the unprecedented act, for a British officer, of swinging a pick with the laborers.

A delegation of Eskimos indicated to the captain that the five deserters from the previous trip were still alive. They carried back a letter from Frobisher urging the sailors to return. He sent pen, ink, and paper for their reply, but he heard nothing. And naturally not. For, if we can believe the Eskimo folk tale that persisted to modern times, the English renegade sailors preferred their life among savages to Frobisher's idea of taut discipline and the prevailing level of British seagoing "comforts" on an Arctic voyage.

On August 21, 1577, the fleet sailed for home with 200 tons of ore.

At home, furnaces smelted the ore and produced, from somewhere, a promising quantity of gold. Since nobody else has ever found profitable quantities of gold in the Meta Incognita, cynical moderns can only suspect chicanery, a lode salted by unknown confidence men for the delusion of suckers.

The trick worked. Next year, Frobisher sailed at the head of a 15-ship fleet.

On July 2, 1578, within sight of Resolution Island, the 100-ton *Dennys* hit an iceberg and sank with the whole fleet as witness. Other ships pressed about and saved all hands. But supplies, and a prefabricated lodge intended to support a year-round colony at the mines, sank to the bottom.

A great stream of broken ice poured down on them and a storm sprang up, scattering the fleet. Unwittingly, they had stumbled into Hudson Strait at the height of the turbulent flood of ice escaping from the inland sea, a torrent terrible to behold even from the deck of a modern, ice-strengthened, steel-hulled steamship.

Despite the dangerous ice stream, most of the ships penetrated deep into the straits. The chronicler even reports that they saw the west coast of America, that they had gone through the Northwest Passage, in other words, and were in the Pacific Ocean! (He missed by only 2,500 miles.) So intent was the captain on getting a payload of ore back home, however, that he abandoned further exploration of what he thought was the long-sought-for road to the riches of Cathay and looked instead for Frobisher Bay and the mines of the first two voyages.

Judging from the account of the chronicler, Frobisher had already developed great skill in ice piloting and cleverly slipped his ships through whatever leads of open water appeared, no matter how narrow and tortuous.

On July 31, they arrived at the mines and began getting out the ore. A crew of stonemasons threw up a house, meaning to let it pass the winter as a test of whether it would collapse under the snow or crack in the cold. Peas, meal, and other nonperishable foodstuffs were buried against the return next year.

The fleet began straggling homeward at the end of August, loaded down with ore. The last arrived in England at the beginning of October.

The chronicler reports with great satisfaction that only 40 persons died, a number he felt was not great, considering the dangerous seas they had sailed.

And all to no good.

For the 1,300 tons of ore contained only fool's gold and were dumped into the harbor. Even the geographers did not profit, for, misled by the mischievous map of Zeno, they placed Frobisher Bay and the Meta Incognita in Greenland. It was not till 1860 that Charles Francis Hall, an American eccentric with a streak of genius as an Arctic explorer, heard from the Eskimos of Baffin Island startlingly accurate accounts of the visit of Frobisher's men three centuries before, including the report on the fate of the five deserters. He also found ruins of the stone house built to test the winter's effects. He definitely placed Frobisher's landfall and mines in the North American Arctic.

Frobisher himself never returned to the northland. He shot upward in the navy and commanded a ship almost equal in size to the vessels of John Hawkins and Francis Drake in the repulse of the Spanish Armada. He was killed in 1594 in a petty skirmish at Brest, France.

Despite the collapse of the gold rush, English merchants continued to dream of a quick way to the East across the top of the world. Just seven years after cleanup crews dumped Frobisher's worthless ore into the harbor, John Davis fitted out two small ships, called poetically the *Sunshine* and the *Moonshine*, and rounded Greenland to sail up the west coast as far as the Arctic Circle, where he turned west, crossed to the Baffin Island coast, and turned south to Cumberland Sound. After probing up the sound about 120 miles (any opening in the North American wall roused hopes that it would pierce clean through to the western sea), Davis turned for home and reached Dartmouth in late September 1585.

The body of water between Greenland and Baffin Island boxed in by his journeys has been named Davis Strait.

On his second voyage, Davis poked along the Baffin Island and Labrador coasts. He lost two sailors of a landing party in an Indian ambush and almost immediately sailed for home.

During the third voyage in 1587, Davis beat up the west coast of Greenland to 73° north. Had he turned west there, as he had on earlier voyages, he would have crossed the mysterious North Water, a perpetually ice-free sea in north Baffin Bay, and discovered the entrance to Lancaster Sound, the true entrance to the Northwest Passage. And Davis knew a great opportunity had been dandled before him, for he wrote of it to one of his patrons.

"I have been in 73 degrees, finding the sea all open and forty leagues between land and land. The passage is most probable, the execution easy."

Except that the distance between "land and land" is considerably more than his estimate, Davis had made a shrewd judgment of the lay of the land. But he never returned to exploit his discovery. His mariner's skills were commandeered by the Royal Navy for the war against Spain.

HUDSON

In 1602 the East India Company rigged out a 52-ton barque for another probe at the North American wall, under command of George Weymouth. His expedition penetrated a short distance into Hudson Strait before the captain turned back for home under threat of a mutiny led by the chaplain, of all people. His trip was of minor importance except that his little ship, the 55-ton oaken *Discovery*, became the greatest Arctic exploration vessel of all time, serving some of the most brilliant pilots and captains of Arctic history in six northern voyages through unknown waters.

Infected with the Arctic madness that seizes the most improbable victims, an unknown mariner named Henry Hudson plagued the merchant adventurers of London with a scheme to quit fooling around with Northwest Passages and sail instead directly for the Pole, straight north from England. Because in those days everybody believed in one of those persistent falsehoods that survive despite a lack of scientific proof—the idea that the polar seas away from coastlines were ice-free—Hudson sold his plan and sailed north to the almost incredible level of 80°; and he did it on the perpetually ice-locked east coast of Greenland, a voyage that would give pause to the skipper of a modern icebreaker.

Although forced to turn back, Hudson refused to go home empty-handed, so he made a little side excursion and found the great whaling grounds around Spitsbergen. His discovery of one of the great whaling areas of all time, ironically, did him out of a patron, for the company got so excited about the profits from whaling that they lost all interest in further exploration—and in the skipper who had found their bonanza.

So Hudson hired out to the Dutch and sailed west in the rickety *Half Moon* to look for a passage through the middle of North America. He sailed up a great river that now bears his name. At the level of present-day Albany, Hudson decided he was getting nowhere.

On his return, he and his crew were arrested by English merchants who had had their feelings hurt because he had worked for foreigners instead of languishing at home in patriotic poverty. Somehow he persuaded them not only to let him go but to found another expedition into the ice, this time to the straits that Davis and Weymouth thought might exist just south of Frobisher's Resolution Island. They gave him Weymouth's sturdy old *Discovery* and a crew of 22. He sailed for the straits on April 17, 1610.

From the beginning, the trip was plagued by troublemakers. Robert Juet, the mate, and a mysterious young man named Henry Greene who came aboard surreptitiously without the knowledge of the owners, displayed a genius for setting their shipmates at each other's throats. And the master himself, for once, didn't seem to have a firm grasp of his job.

The *Discovery* entered the vast inland sea of Hudson Bay and wandered about its interior to no apparent purpose, through the summer and dangerously late into autumn.

In September Hudson called an extraordinary kind of captain's mast at which he himself seems to have been the accused, charged by his mate Juet with a list of wrongdoings. Martin Frobisher would have put up with such a proceeding just long enough to bend a musket barrel around Juet's head. The crew came to the master's defense, but the whole affair shows a shocking lack of leadership.

The captain did depose Juet and named a Robert Bylot in

his place, but soon afterward replaced that skillful pilot and navigator with an unlettered brute from the forecastle, a sailor of no education or nautical skill.

By October the *Discovery* was frozen in at the southern end of James Bay, a cul-de-sac about as unhandy for escape as exists within 1,000 miles. Hudson's was the first ship forced to winter in the Arctic ice. The curious collapse of capacity in the onetime master seaman showed glaringly when the crew learned that the master had allowed his ship to be trapped for the winter knowing he had brought only a few months' provisions, though there had been room to bring much more. By spring Hudson's men were eating moss. More ominous, the Englishmen stooped to eating frogs, a dish an Englishman eats only in his last extremity—if then. Failure of the tea supply, also a catastrophe for Englishmen, was partly repaired by the ship's surgeon, who brewed a kind of turpentine tea from spruce buds.

Henry Greene and Juet organized a mutiny and took the ship from the captain. They put him, his seven-year-old son, and seven loyal (or sick) sailors over the side in a small shallop with one musket, a little powder and shot, an iron pot, and some meal. Hudson and his fellows were never seen again.

On the way out of the bay, the crew tried to trade with Eskimos but were ambushed and lost five men, including Greene, the ringleader.

Before heading home, the survivors had the good sense to rename the able Robert Bylot as master. Juet, the original and senior mate, died anyhow, of starvation—and no wonder, for they were living on wild-goose bones fried in candle tallow with vinegar, each man receiving half a pound of candles weekly.

On their return they were arrested, naturally, but were acquitted by a board of inquiry that reported the shocking and apparently true testimony that the mutineers had found a hatch cut between the captain's cabin and the hold so that

Hudson could keep himself, his son, and his favorites well fed while the crew suffered on starvation rations.

The mutineers must have been persuasive, for Robert Bylot, their homeward-bound pilot, commanded the *Discovery* again on a mission supposedly to rescue Hudson. And in 1615 Bylot took the stout old *Discovery* out again to poke about Foxe Channel, north of Hudson Bay, looking for a way west. His pilot, or what we now call a chief officer, was a William Baffin, who enjoyed a happy blend of talents as superb mathematician-navigator and chronicler.

BYLOT AND BAFFIN

The Foxe Channel trip didn't turn up much, but it exercised a team of mariners, Robert Bylot and William Baffin, who left England again the next spring of 1616. (It was only four years later that the *Mayflower* would cross the Atlantic, carrying the Pilgrims to Plymouth Rock.)

Bylot's experiences in Hudson Bay and adjacent waters had not encouraged him, so they tried going farther north. In one of the most extraordinary ice voyages in history, the stout little *Discovery* fought through the dangerous ice of Baffin Bay, through the great assemblage of icebergs in Melville Bay, by Thule, Greenland, where the United States now operates its farthest northern air base, to the mouth of Smith Sound at 78° north. The ship rounded the top of Baffin Bay and came down the west coast, the coast of the Queen Elizabeth Islands in the Canadian archipelago. Bylot and Baffin headed the first white party in that region since the shadowy Viking hunters who hundreds of years earlier had left the eider-duck shelters behind.

The party passed the mouth of Jones Sound, but not without naming and noting it for future study.

And they passed Lancaster Sound, the entrance to the Northwest Passage they were seeking. They pressed on down the west coast of North America. When they reached familiar waters already explored by earlier voyages, they crossed the Atlantic to home, thus ending their careers and the career of a great ship as Arctic explorers, but not before recording one of the most brilliant voyages in history.

Credit for the masterly handling of the *Discovery* must go to Robert Bylot. William Baffin, armed with newly invented instruments, made astronomical observations and notes on the earth's magnetism, ice patterns, tides and currents, and Arctic anthropology that should have advanced polar navigation and science by enormous leaps.

But they didn't.

Probably because Robert Bylot still bore the stigma of having guided Hudson's mutineers home, his name was forgotten almost immediately.

Like the mean-spirited Greeks who dismissed the voyage of Pytheas as a hoax, the warmwater sailors of the admiralty scoffed at Baffin's pretensions. For 200 years, admiralty charts showed blank the area north of Davis's last discoveries, with the note: "*Baffin's Bay according to the relation of W. Baffin in 1616, but not now believed.*"

For those 200 years, no sailors had the skill and courage to sail the waters which Bylot had plied and which Baffin had charted so exquisitely that the later rediscoverers of his bay were lavish with praise for his skill.

So closed the age of innocence when hardy seamen, English mostly and blissfully ignorant of the dangers of sailing through the murderous ice fields of Arctic seas, ventured into them in vessels scarcely able to stand up to a real tempest in open sea. But those innocents made a tremendous record.

Beginning with Frobisher in 1576 through the Baffin-Bylot

voyage in 1616, merchant sailors in 40 years charted the east coast of Canada and western Greenland to 78° north, a vast and hostile region approached with caution even by today's ice-strengthened vessels.

Recognition has come belatedly for the great of that period. One of the world's largest islands is named for Baffin. The strait between Labrador and Greenland bears Davis's name. A major jet base serving the Canadian Arctic lies at the head of Frobisher Bay. A river and an immense bay carry Hudson's name.

The first time I sailed into Lancaster Sound and our ship came to grips with the true bottleneck of the Northwest Passage, I was overwhelmed by the beauty of an ice-covered mountain soaring 6,000 feet high on the southern shore. Low-skimming light of the weak Arctic sun painted the ice cap salmon and apricot hues; occasional broken edges, catching the sun's rays, flashed streaks of dazzling white fire.

It is Bylot Island, and it stands precisely where it should to honor the great sailor of the age of innocence.

Chapter 3

THE HARD DEATH OF ANIAN

Caribou and Birds by Pitseolak

The Sea Dwellers by Kalvak

Characteristically, posterity rejected soundly documented discoveries like Bylot's and Baffiin's while clinging to belief in a mythical passage supposedly discovered in 1500 by Gaspar Cortereal and named the Strait of Anian. The hoax was reinforced in 1588 by a Spaniard named Maldonado. According to the legend, this tantalizing Strait of Anian crossed North America from the west shore of Hudson Bay to the Gulf of Alaska, emptying into the Pacific at a conveniently all-seasons-navigable latitude of 60° north.

Unsupported by sound navigational data as the Maldonado claim was, it would possibly—though not certainly—have soon died, except for an unfortunate boost the story got in 1596. A brilliant English merchant-adventurer, sea captain, and stout believer in the Northwest Passage named Michael Lok traveled to Venice on business and there heard a story that reawakened belief in the Strait of Anian.

Although he had been badly stung 18 years earlier as the chief sponsor of the Frobisher gold-mining fiasco, Lok still had great wealth and widespread business interests. And he also had an unsquelchable faith in the Northwest Passage, for he allowed himself to be buttonholed by an Ancient Mariner of Cephalonia, Greece, who spun a fascinating tale of Arctic discovery. His yarn, spread by the excited Lok, had the same inexplicable vitality as the Zeno hoax and, like that fabrication, was destined to work mischief among Arctic adventurers for almost 200 years.

The 61-year-old Apostolos Valerianus told Lok that for 40

years, under the name of Juan de Fuca, he had piloted Spanish ships about the New World. Just four years previously, the Greek said, he had piloted two ships from Mexico up the Pacific coast in search of the western opening of the Strait of Anian.

At about 47° north on the Pacific coast, he said, he had penetrated a wide channel leading deep into the continental landmass. At the entrance to the channel stood a pillar of rock, making an unmistakable landmark. For 20 days his flotilla had sailed between a belt of islands and a mainland rich in gold. The channel ended in the Arctic Sea.

The Greek sailor offered to pilot an English expedition to this Strait of Anian. For a price, of course—60,000 ducats. The eager English merchant-adventurer raced home to solicit help but was unable to raise the money. When he returned to Greece to bargain with Juan de Fuca, he found that the old sailor had died.

But the Greek's story of discovering a western opening to the Strait of Anian did not die with him. It lived for almost 200 years and lured dozens of brave men to their death.

(Virtually all historians assume Juan de Fuca was a confidence man and Michael Lok a gullible victim. In fairness I would like to point out, however, that a pillar of rock marks the entrance to a vast strait—called Strait of Juan de Fuca—just a few miles north of his supposed discovery. And a vessel entering that channel and sailing for 20 days would be bent northward through an inland sea between an archipelago of islands and the mainland. That channel is now called the Inside Passage. And the vessel would come out into the Gulf of Alaska exactly where some of the world's mightiest glaciers calve thousands of icebergs, giving an illusion of Arctic austerity. It is just possible that the old Greek sea dog may have made the trip and merely been more of a sloppy navigator than a rogue.)

After Baffin's discouraging words about prospects of finding an opening to the Northwest Passage in the Far North, the search shifted to the latitude of Maldonado's Strait of Anian, which happens to coincide closely with the entrance to Hudson Bay. Henry Hudson had explored only the eastern shore, leaving open to discovery the exciting possibilities of the western waters, where the passage would naturally be located.

In 1619 Christian IV, the Danish Sailor King, equipped a two-ship expedition to probe the western reaches of Hudson Bay. To lead the flotilla he chose Jens Munk, a 40-year-old sailor of fortune who had free-lanced as a merchant sailor in Portugal and Brazil while still a growing boy, had served with the Dutch, had owned a merchant vessel before he was 25, and had explored the waters in the polar seas north of Siberia. He had fought the Swedes as a captain in the Danish navy and had broken up a pirates' nest off the coast of Norway. When King Christian looked for a bold sailor of large experience in icy waters, his sea lords called his attention to Captain Munk, who had just returned from establishing a Danish whaling industry in Spitsbergen.

On May 9, 1619, Munk sailed with the ship *Unicorn* and the sloop *Lamprey*. Munk's expedition led to no important discoveries, certainly not to the nonexistent Strait of Anian, but he left a journal revealing an unexpectedly noble spirit in a man of so turbulent a history—a journal almost unequaled in the literature of exploration for harrowing detail of suffering and death.

Scarcely had the two ships and 65 men left Denmark when a sailor jumped overboard and plunged his head under the waves to forestall rescue. Most of the rest of the crew would have been wise to follow him.

Their travail began at the mouth to Hudson Strait. Beginning on July 8, 1619, the two ships inched westward through gales and grinding ice floes, taking 41 days to reach Digges Islands, only 450 miles in from the sea. In two more weeks they had crossed the great bay to the western shore where Churchill now stands. By then, winter was closing in fast, so Munk beached his ships and dug them in to keep them from being carried away by drift ice. He issued winter clothing, built fireplaces, threw up protective earthworks about his ships, set watches, and assigned firewood and water details. The generous-spirited Munk rationed their store of whiskey and Spanish wine, but allowed the men as much beer as they wished. With this little hitch: The beer froze to the bottom of the barrels and he required the sailors to boil it before drinking to prevent some vaguely suspected bad effect on health.

On November 10, 1619, St. Martin's Eve, Munk celebrated a Danish holiday by serving ptarmigan instead of the traditional goose and issuing a pint of wine beyond the normal allowance. He described his crew as "merry and joyful." On Christmas Eve he gave his men wine and strong beer, "as much as they could stand," and they became sprightly despite the cold and almost daylong darkness outside. They devised games to play on the ice for whiling away the days, and their commander reported himself well satisfied with their condition. On New Year's Day the temperature plummeted and Munk gave every man two pints of wine over his usual allowance.

Then on January 10 came an ominous warning. The chaplain and surgeon quit fighting back against a malaise that had dragged at them for weeks, and they took to their beds. Soon, the head cook died.

Each day more members of the expedition showed the dreaded signs of scurvy, a hideous affliction that was the scourge of seagoing men till modern times.

Recognizable symptoms of scurvy occur in the Ebers papyrus, written in 1500 B.C. Hippocrates describes the disease, and many historians blame scurvy for the failure of the Crusades. In 1753 James Lind, an English ship's surgeon, wrote an excellent paper and prescribed daily dosage with citrus juices—whence the slang term of "Limeys" for English sailors, a contraction of "lime-juicers." But acceptance of Dr. Lind's theory was slow and not universal. Besides, even the largest stores of lime juice eventually become useless, for they lose their potency with age.

Scurvy comes from lack of Vitamin C. The body stores of Vitamin C leach out rapidly, but symptoms of scurvy do not appear for about six months. The Munk expedition had enjoyed a few meals of fresh meat rich in Vitamin C, notably a polar bear shot on the ice, and so had put off appearance of the disease for a month. But just seven months after they had left home and existed on a diet of vitamin-impoverished salt meat, boiled beer, and wine, the dreaded symptoms began to appear.

Complaining of aching joints and muscles, the icebound sailors fell into depression and abnormal fatigue. The skin, especially on the legs, turned black as though badly bruised. Fevers ran high. Blood pressure dropped. Gums swelled into purple masses; eventually they closed over the teeth and hid them under pads of stinking flesh painfully engorged with blood. Then gangrene attacked the gums and the teeth fell out. Small hemorrhages in the brain brought on confusion, convulsions, coma, and death.

Munk's journal through the bitter winter months of January, February, and March of 1620 is a tragic litany of death. Each entry concerned itself almost entirely with that day's burials. Till one day nobody was strong enough to bury the dead, and they lay where they fell.

Despairing of survival, Munk wrote a last message to the world and took to his bunk. Two of his men went ashore to flee the charnel-house atmosphere of the death ship. By June 8, Munk could no longer stand the stench of the dead and dragged himself on deck. The sailors ashore, who had given up their commander for dead, saw him moving about the deck and carried him to the beach. There the trio crawled about on hands and knees, devouring each sprig of green that poked up through the melting snow.

Ghastly as scurvy is, the disease yields dramatically to treatment. One fresh orange, for instance, and the worst case will show startling improvement within two days. Gums begin to heal, and within two weeks scarcely a trace of skin discoloration or muscular weakness remains. The fresh greens of the subarctic spring landscape put the three survivors back on their feet. They set nets for fish, shot birds, and, as health improved, worked on the *Lamprey* to float it and rig for the long voyage home. On July 16, 1620, they sailed, but gales and drifting ice hindered the undermanned sloop and did not release them at the exit from Hudson Strait into the open sea till the 14th of August, 1620.

On September 20, they sailed into a Norwegian fjord and at gunpoint forced a surly peasant to lead them to safety. Of the 65 men who had left Denmark in search of the Strait of Anian, 3 returned.

Incredibly, the doughty Jens Munk set about planning an immediate return to the scene of his nightmare. But the Thirty Years War raged and the Danish king needed a sailor of Munk's stature in his navy. Munk rose to admiral of the Danish navy and died at 49, with the highest naval honors his country could give. But he died a disappointed man, for he had never been able to return to the Arctic in quest of the elusive Strait of Anian.

Other mariners did not show the eagerness of the intrepid Dane to return to the icy wastes of Hudson Bay, but by 1631 rival merchants of London and Bristol mounted expeditions to search the western shore of Hudson Bay. A Yorkshire coastal pilot named Luke Foxe headed the London venture in the pinnace *Charles*. Foxe showed the keen sense of public relations that seems as necessary to lasting fame for an explorer as does accomplishment. He insisted, for instance, on calling himself

"Northwest" Foxe. The leader of the Bristol band, on the other hand, was Thomas James, a wealthy gentleman-attorney of charming manner and gentle disposition. He sailed in the 70-ton *Henrietta Maria*.

Both ships penetrated to the western shore of Hudson Bay and by an extraordinary coincidence encountered each other in that vast, near-empty waste. The gentlemanly James invited Captain Foxe and his officers to dinner aboard the *Henrietta Maria*. The two companies exchanged notes about their discoveries, which had been meager enough, and parted company the next day.

As winter approached, Captain Foxe noted the first signs of scurvy and hurried home "not having lost one Man, nor Boy, nor any manner of Tackling, having been forth neere 6 months, all glory be to God."

What Captain Foxe did not know was that scurvy takes just about six months to strike and he had slipped home just under the wire.

Not so the gallant Captain James, who wintered over in Hudson Bay. His crew, fed only from stores of salt beef, salt pork, dry fish, beans, lentils, and porridge, suffered hideously from scurvy. A principal daytime occupation for his crew was the trimming away of diseased tissue from each other's gums.

With the breakup of ice the following midsummer, the survivors fought their way out of the icy trap of Hudson Bay and escaped into the open sea on September 3, 1632. They reached Bristol on October 22.

Sometime after Capt. James's return, the ungenerous Foxe repaid James's Arctic hospitality by publicly ridiculing his competence.

". . . The Gentleman could discourse of Arte," Foxe wrote, "and shewed me many Instruments, so that I did perceive him to bee a practitioner in the Mathematicks; but, when I found that hee was no Seaman, I did blame those very much who had councelled him to make choyce of that shippe for a voyage of such importance. . . ."

An objective assessment of the accomplishments of the two yields about the same credit to both. Between them they had searched virtually the entire western shore of Hudson and James bays and had found no opening to a Strait of Anian.

Their lack of success effectively cooled the Northwest Passage fever among Europe's mariners for decades. But the lure of the Strait of Anian persisted and the search shifted landward.

Two renegade French fur traders defected from New France to England, where they persuaded Prince Rupert and a band of hard-bargaining merchant adventurers to get a charter in 1670 for the "Governor and Company of Adventurers, trading into Hudson's Bay"—commonly known then and now as the Hudson's Bay Company. The king charged them with searching for the Northwest Passage but also granted a monopoly on trading in the region, a clause of the charter that fascinated the founders far more than the opportunity to gain fame as explorers. The company's agents set up forts for trading with the Indians and ran their affairs as though Hudson Bay were a private pond.

But on the throne of France at the time sat Louis XIV, the Sun King, jealous of any infringement on French *grandeur*, especially in those parts of Canada he considered rightfully French. So he undertook an improbable naval war in the frozen waters of Hudson Bay and soon reduced all but one of the company's forts. In 1697 the king dispatched a flotilla to capture the lone holdout. Aboard was Sieur de la Potherie, a Gallic popinjay, the very model of a comic stage French dandy. His account of the campaign is a delightful exercise in bombast, a gushing fountain of chauvinism and gasconade in brilliant contrast to the dour style of the Anglo-Saxon mariners with their sempiternal sangfroid.

Despite the fact that a steady procession of English sailors had transited Hudson Strait before his day, the French chronicler reported that the storms and ice there were "unconquerable by other people, but only awakened the bravery of the French who . . . find nothing that can repel their attack."

To his astonishment, they filled 40 barrels with fresh water taken from melt pools on the ice. But, like good Frenchmen, they were careful to add brandy to the barrels, for "it would be perilous to drink it" otherwise.

Near the British fort at Port Nelson, the French and a British flotilla fought a savage naval battle. And in clear violation of the conventions of warfare, as understood by the Anglo-Saxon mind, the bombastic French soundly thrashed the taciturn English, inflicting hundreds of casualties and sinking the principal warship. But the French suffered losses of men and ships also, in this first naval battle fought in drifting Arctic ice.

Sieur de la Potherie had his ship shot out from under him and waded ashore with his men, through icy waters and across snow-covered bogs, to lay siege to the fort. After a desultory bombardment by the French, the English surrendered and the French embarked on those ships still afloat, to carry their prisoners and loot back to France.

But the cruel ice fields of the bay held them prisoner and a vicious plague of scurvy broke out. The extravagant Frenchman wrote a lengthy medical analysis of the disease, full of the medieval nonsense of the day about corrosive spirits and viscous humors; but here and there a gleam of brilliance shows through. For instance, he suspected the seaman's standard diet of salt meat to be the cause of the illness and recommended frequent lemon-juice gargles.

While the French were adventuring in the middle high latitudes of Hudson Bay, their compatriots back home were adventuring in the book trade. A Joseph Nicolas Delisle, brother of a distinguished geographer, traded on his brother's reputation by publishing a map in 1750 which showed a channel running eastward from the Pacific in approximately the right place for the elusive Strait of Anian. Supposedly, a Spanish admiral named Bartholomew de Fonte had sailed deep into the passage about 1640. Maps continued to reproduce the mythical passage for many years. And so explorers continued to hope the entrance to the Northwest Passage would be found somewhere near Hudson Bay.

When the French turned their backs, the English slipped back into Hudson Bay and pursued the lucrative fur trade, despite continued harassment by the French. More worrisome than the French were harassments at home by powerful merchants and members of the parliament, who charged that the company was neglecting the search for a Northwest Passage to preserve a monopoly of trade with Indians and Eskimos deliberately kept isolated and ignorant. To still those complaints—and to search for a copper mine of enormous richness reported by Indians to lie at the mouth of a river emptying into Arctic seas—the Hudson's Bay Company dispatched an employee named Samuel Hearne in quest of the Strait of Anian.

This young sailor, who had volunteered for the cross-country trek with only Indians for company, could easily have won the title of Least Likely to Succeed in any poll of Arctic explorers. Shy, gentle, afflicted with a fatal ability to see the other fellow's side in any confrontation, Samuel Hearne had working for him only a quiet stubbornness that drove him to complete any job he started.

He left Churchill the first time on November 6, 1769, and got only 200 miles along the road when his Indian escort abandoned him. He barely made it back to the fort. Undaunted, he set out again in February 1770 and reached Dubawnt Lake, about one-third of the way to the mouth of the Coppermine

River. He set up his quadrant to calculate his latitude and walked off to wait for a cloud to pass from the sun. A gust of wind toppled his tripod, broke the quadrant, and made further progress useless—for without accurate observations it was pointless to suffer further privations and hardships.

Besides, a band of 600 northern Indians soon surrounded Hearne and his 5 Indian companions and stripped them of all their goods. Hearne persuaded them to return a knife, awl, needle, and razor and started home. His companions abandoned him and he had to fight his way home alone through worsening winter weather. Fortunately, in September he encountered an Indian chieftain named Matonabbee, who clothed and fed him and restored his face by giving a feast in his honor. Matonabbee had been to the mouth of the Coppermine River and, when he heard that Hearne stubbornly insisted on a third try, offered to guide him.

He listened to Hearne's account of his first two trials with an expert's critical ear.

The cause of failure he pinpointed quickly.

No women on the first two trips.

"When all the men are heavy laden, they can neither hunt nor travel to any considerable distance; and in case they meet with success in hunting, who is to carry the produce of their labor?"

One woman can carry twice as much as a man, the Indian said. And women eat very little, for in hard times they can get by with merely licking their fingers as they cook.

Hearne spent weeks in the agreeable company of the Indian chief, for whom he developed great respect and affection. In November he set out for home. The weather had grown so bad that Hearne's dog froze to death on the trail, but the stubborn explorer pressed on. He reached Fort Prince of Wales on November 25, 1770.

Hearne had not reached the Coppermine River or settled the problem of the Strait of Anian, and many historians dismiss his second trip as a failure. But he had made an extraordinary voyage across 120,000 square miles of subarctic wilderness, mapping as he went, and had kept a notebook of natural history that still makes profitable reading. Lewis and Clark and Zebulon Pike have won lasting fame for voyages much less demanding.

Hearne's employers must have been satisfied, for they raised his salary. And the governor of the fort authorized immediate organization of a third expedition.

Hearne put his Indian friend in charge of gathering supplies and personnel—including enough women to do the heavy work and keep the hunters warm at night. Matonabbee had wives cached all over the north country, but he took three women along as wives in permanent residence.

Less than two weeks after stumbling in from the second voyage, Hearne left the fort again for the third assault on the legendary copper mines and the Strait of Anian. Matonabbee did not head straight into the treeless Barren Lands that lay across the road to the Coppermine River, but took a longer route through the forest for the shelter and game to be found there.

The small party ran into nomadic tribes. The wandering warriors, on learning of their destination, immediately attached themselves to Hearne's party so they could massacre Coppermine Eskimos on some imaginary pretext. Hearne protested and Matonabbee spoke up for the Eskimos, saying they had treated him generously on his previous visit to their country. But the savage warriors overruled them brusquely and seem to have taken control of the expedition.

Despite the cruel cold of the Canadian interior, the party pressed northwestward toward the unsuspecting Eskimos.

One of Matonabbee's wives froze her buttocks so severely

that they were encrusted with frost rime. When they thawed, blisters as large as footballs prevented her sitting. Her fellow Indians thought her accident an uproarious joke, for she was a notorious flirt who wore her skirts too short for the approval of the other redskin girls. Hearne allowed himself a prim note of censure.

"I must acknowledge that I was not in the number of those who pitied her, as I thought she took too much pains to shew a clean heel and a good leg; her garters being always in sight. . . ."

(At the U.S. Army laboratory of Arctic medicine in Fairbanks, Alaska, I have seen photographs of the terrible ravages worked on pretty derrieres by the unwise coquetry of wearing miniskirts in a subarctic clime. Unlike the prissy Mr. Hearne, I had to wince in sympathy for the unfortunate girls, flirts or no.)

Along the trail, Hearne made an important first step in Arctic exploration. Not only did he learn to eat the native diet, but actually relished a mass of mosses and lichens taken from a caribou's stomach and fermented; unborn fawn; unhatched birds; and other native dainties. And he showed no sign of scurvy!

With our invaluable hindsight, it is hard to understand how generations of European explorers starved and died of scurvy in a land that had supported thousands of generations of Indians and Eskimos in rollicking good health. It was only after Arctic explorers followed Hearne's example and went native that scurvy was banished and the threat of starvation sharply reduced.

On July 15, 1771, the party stood on the Coppermine River near its mouth. The Indians painted their war shields with mystic designs, crossed the river to the east bank, and crept up on an Eskimo village of five tents found by scouts five miles downstream. Shortly after midnight of July 17, the Indians descended on the sleeping village. Twenty or more naked Eskimos ran from the tents and were cut down savagely. A young girl was skewered at Hearne's feet, but did not die quickly. Hearne ordered the Indians to kill her or he would, and a thrust through the heart cut short her suffering.

When the Eskimo band was exterminated, the Indians looted the tents and destroyed what they could not carry off.

(The cruel warfare between Eskimo and Indian, along the cultural face that separates them, has left scars to this day. Near the Chukchi Sea in Alaska, I once saw uncontrollable terror seize the women of an Eskimo village when a maiden ran through the streets screaming that she had seen Indians hiding in the tundra nearby. Even after their men, who certainly knew the Indian raiders were figments of an unhealthy fantasy, had swept the tundra for miles about, the women jibbered with fright for hours.)

As soon as Hearne felt the Indians had become sated and ready to listen to reason, he proposed completion of the main purpose of the trip.

Eight miles downstream Hearne came to the shores of what is now called Coronation Gulf and found the river blocked by sandbars and ice, useless for navigation.

Hearne stood on the shore, gazing over the icy wastes stretching northward, fully conscious of the historical importance of the moment. For he was the first white man to reach Arctic waters between the east coast of Baffin Island and the eastern tip of Siberia. And he had killed for good the dream of the Strait of Anian.

Eighteen years later, Alexander Mackenzie, an employee of the rival North West Company, arrived at the mouth of the Mackenzie River almost 500 miles west along the Arctic shoreline, and his employers noisily promoted his trip as having killed for all time belief in the Strait of Anian. Mackenzie was a brilliant explorer and his notebooks have been invaluable contribu-

tions to knowledge of the Arctic, but no serious mariner had
believed in a channel through the North American landmass
since Hearne had crossed the northland from south to north
without encountering a waterway suitable for westbound traffic.

The search for the Northwest Passage fell again into neglect.

Chapter 4

FAME, KNOWLEDGE, DEATH, BUT LITTLE RICHES

Sea Monsters Devouring Whale by Kiakshuk

November Ravens by Lizzie

When the English explorer-sailor Capt. James Cook sailed through Bering Strait and around the shoulder of Alaska in 1778, he found a vast field of polar ice pressing down on the coastline and cutting off the route eastward. He reported that no Northwest Passage existed south of 70° north, and that the seas north of that latitude remained frozen and thus were useless for trade. Captain Cook's report killed what little hope remained for a commercially useful shortcut across the top of the world. And Europe soon became locked in the titanic struggle of the Napoleonic Wars, leaving little energy for adventuring in the ice.

But Napoleon finally fell at Waterloo in 1815, and England faced the problem of what to do with an unemployed navy and the restless energies of victorious but idle sailors.

In 1817 a whaling captain of great renown for his daring voyages into the Arctic reported to the Royal Society that the Arctic climate was moderating and the ice moving northward. This William Scoresby enlisted the help of the famed naturalist Sir Joseph Banks, president of the society, to urge the English to make another attempt at the Northwest Passage.

To replace the hope of finding riches through opening a new route for commerce, a hope dashed by Captain Cook, the parliament offered a sliding scale of pound-sterling rewards for ice exploration: for ships reaching 83° north, £1,000; for reaching 85°, £2,000; for reaching 88°, £4,000; and for reaching 89°, £5,000. Rewards for westward travel at high latitudes were even greater: for reaching 110° west above the Arctic Circle, £5,000; for reaching the Mackenzie River delta, £10,000; for reaching 150° west (almost exactly the longitude, coincidentally, of the Alaskan North Slope oil fields at Prudhoe Bay), £15,000; and for reaching the Pacific Ocean, £20,000, a very handsome sum for those days.

The incentives were more than enough for British mariners chafing in the idleness imposed by peace. The navy immediately began mounting two expeditions; one was to try for the Northwest Passage and the other was to sail straight north across the Pole.

Shipyards strengthened four whaling vessels with athwartships oaken beams, exterior oak sheathing, and armor-plated prows. Beds replaced hammocks, tailors sewed fur-lined clothes for all hands, food for three years jammed the holds.

Persisting in the delusion that ice formed only near shorelines and the polar seas were ice-free, the navy ordered two of the vessels to sail north with the hope of crossing the Pole to Bering Strait and the Pacific Ocean. That expedition soon discovered the polar ice pack was very real and impregnable, even far from Greenland's shore. They returned to England with small results.

The other pair of ships sailed in April to the tip of Greenland and up Davis Strait, headed for latitude 70° and even north of there, if necessary. The expedition leader, Capt. John Ross, rode *Isabella*, and his second-in-command, Lt. William Edward Parry, rode *Alexander*.

Following almost exactly in the 200-year-old wake of Bylot-Baffin's *Discovery*, the flotilla coasted northward, picking up whalers along the way till they had formed a 42-ship convoy. Ross and Parry recognized with delight landmarks described by Baffin. (Even as Ross was verifying the brilliance of the work of a colleague two centuries dead, two books appeared in

England with entries dismissing Baffin's work as "not now believed.") With a generosity characteristic of the man, Ross
wrote a vindication of the wronged explorer.

"In rediscovering Baffin's Bay, I have derived great addi-
tional pleasure from the reflection that I have placed in a fair
light before the Public all the merits of a worthy and able Navigator; whose fate, like that of many others, it has not only been,
to have lost . . . the opportunity of acquiring during his lifetime
the fame he deserved; but, could he have lived to this period, to
have seen . . . the bay, with which his name is so fairly associ-
ated, treated as a phantom of the imagination."

Ross's own reputation as a mariner was just about to suffer
a setback.

After rounding the top of Baffin Bay and sailing southwest
along the eastern edge of the Canadian Arctic archipelago, Ross
turned into Lancaster Sound and penetrated some distance
without encountering ice.

Ross had no way of knowing, but he had discovered the Northwest Passage, and eternal fame lay ahead.

Inexplicably, he turned about, saying that the waterway was
only an inlet, closed a few miles ahead by a towering range he
named Croker's Mountains.

Controversy raged for years about Ross's failure to transit
Lancaster Sound. His second-in-command, Lieutenant Parry,
said later that he was nonplussed by the order to turn about.
Many officers reported they could see no mountain barrier
ahead.

But most of the politicians and other landlubbers who con-
demned John Ross have never sailed in Arctic waters, so they
know nothing of the weirdly shifting mirages that give the landscape a constantly changing shape, hanging whole fields of icebergs upside-down in the sky, stacking images of distant coastlines two and three deep above the horizon. A phantom mountain

range closing a waterway can come and go a dozen times a day in those high latitudes.

Parry later wrote his opinion of the navigability of Lancaster Sound—and perhaps here the significant word is "later":

". . . I was not sanguine, formerly, as to the existence of a northwest passage, or as to the practicability of it, if it did exist. But our voyage to this Lancaster Sound, as Baffin calls it, has left quite a different impression, for it has not only given us every reason to believe that it is a broad passage into some sea to the westward (probably that of Hearne and Mackenzie); but what is more important still, that it is, at certain seasons, practicable; for, when we were here, there was not a bit of ice to be seen."

On returning home, the young lieutenant did not hesitate to blurt his belief that "on our late voyage, we entered a magnificent strait, from thirty to sixty miles wide, upon the west coast of Baffin's Bay, and—came out again, nobody knows why."

If Parry was scuttling the reputation of his superior to further his own career, he succeeded admirably. Within months he was given the 375-ton bomb vessel *Hecla* and the 180-ton gun brig *Griper* to try for Bering Strait by way of Lancaster Sound. And Ross never again received an important mission from the Royal Navy, for in navy circles, at least, his reputation was irredeemably destroyed.

But there is indication of the genuine competence of Ross— and of his generous and kindly nature—in the final entry of his report:

"Not an instance of punishment has taken place in this ship, nor has there been an officer, or man, in the sick list; and it is with a feeling not to be expressed, that I . . . conclude this letter, by reporting that the service has been performed, and the expedition, I had the honour to command, has returned, without the loss of a man."

Few captains in those days of barbarously cruel discipline and careless or stupid medical service could make such a statement.

Parry's expedition left England May 11, 1819, and by June 18 was in the ice of Davis Strait. He pressed northward, hugging the Greenland coast to avoid the great pack that blocks the Baffin Island coast. Reaching the latitude of Lancaster Sound, Parry turned westward and sailed through the Baffin pack to open water on the west side.

"Sir James Lancaster's Sound was now open to the westward of us, and the experience of our former voyage had given us reason to believe that the best two months of the year for the navigation of these seas were yet to come. . . . We were now about to enter and to explore that great sound or inlet which has obtained a degree of celebrity beyond what it might otherwise have been considered to possess, from the very opposite opinions which have been held with regard to it. . . . It is more easy to imagine than to describe the almost breathless anxiety which was now visible in every countenance, while, as the breeze increased to a fresh gale, we ran quickly up the Sound."

Parry made one detour south into Prince Regent Inlet but was turned back by ice. From then on, his progress was unerringly down the westward path later plotted as the only feasible route for deep draft commercial vessels.

That deep draft route runs almost straight west, lined on both sides by grim Arctic islands with many channels leading almost straight north and south out of the main channel. That central route, like a street in Paris, keeps a continuous, uninterrupted course westward but changes its name every few miles, beginning as Lancaster Sound and becoming Barrow Strait and Viscount Melville Sound. At the western end of Viscount Melville Sound, the channel forks around Banks Island, farthest southwestward of the Canadian Arctic islands. Beyond lies the

Beaufort Sea, an outer fringe of the Arctic Ocean that carries wind-driven floating ice packs of the frozen polar fields.

Straight westward at the end of Viscount Melville Sound, the broad reaches of M'Clure Strait stretch invitingly. Turning southward along the eastern shore of Banks Island is a narrower, less-exciting-looking channel called Prince of Wales Strait. Parry had no way of knowing that M'Clure stays plugged by a stupendous ice jam blown in by prevailing westerlies from the polar seas, but that Prince of Wales Strait catches only a little finger of the jam at the northern end because it is protected from the westerlies in the lee of Banks Island. So he chose the ice-jammed M'Clure Strait.

Parry was elated by his western progress and said he was "finally disentangled from the land which forms the western side of Baffin's Bay; and that, in fact, we had actually entered the Polar Sea. . . ."

He hadn't entered the polar sea, and he himself finally guessed correctly that he was sailing through an archipelago, because winds held north-south or east-west courses, indicating that he was sailing through crosshatch wind channels between islands.

On September 6, 1819, he made a note that his command had crossed "the meridian of 110° west from Greenwich, in the latitude of 74° 44' 20" N.; by which His Majesty's ships, under my orders, became entitled to the sum of five thousand pounds being the reward offered by the King's order . . . to such of His Majesty's subjects as might succeed in penetrating thus far to the westward within the Arctic Circle."

Parry pushed on, but winter was coming down fast from the Pole and the ice thickened till he was forced to turn back on September 18, 1819, at 112° 51' west.

After that unprecedented dash westward, Parry and his men sawed a canal through seven-inch fresh ice in a protected spot on the south shore of Melville Island. Parry named the wintering site Winter Harbour. High-spirited over their triumphant westward journey and fully confident of collecting the £20,000 for reaching the Pacific by that same season next year, the mariners rigged sails on the blocks of ice sawed adrift in the canal and rode them out to sea.

During the long winter, the crews kept up spirits with theatrical performances. The officers published *The North Georgia Gazette and Winter Chronicle*. When they found that only three of the ordinary seamen could read it with any comfort, they organized classes to teach reading and writing.

Parry had brought along a large store of the antiscorbutics of the day, but supplemented them with mustard and cress grown in boxes on the ship's heating pipes. His men suffered only minor annoyance from scurvy.

In May they began to saw their way out again. Winter Harbour was ice-free by August 1, 1820, and the flotilla sailed westward. But in less than two weeks they turned back again, defeated by the dense polar pack driven by prevailing westerly winds from the Beaufort Sea into the funnel of M'Clure Strait and jammed into a 220-mile-long ice plug. They turned about at 113° 46′ 43″, a record of westward penetration of M'Clure Strait that stood for 149 years and then was barely surpassed by the S.S. *Manhattan* that used its mighty 43,000-horsepower turbines to advance only about 50 miles farther than the sail flotilla.

By October 30, 1820, the Parry expedition was home, after completing one of the most brilliant voyages of Arctic exploration of all time. His flotilla had sailed to within 200 miles of breaking out into the Beaufort Sea.

Parry returned to the Arctic in 1821 with the familiar *Hecla* and a sister ship *Fury*. Despite his previous year's success in the northern deep draft channel, he seems to have been daunted by the truly formidable ice of M'Clure Strait, for on his return he looked for a more southerly channel through the tangle of bays and inlets in Foxe Basin. Those waters had already been explored unsuccessfully for a Northwest Passage. He spent three summers sailing and 310 winter days frozen in the same floe and arrived home with notebooks brimming and miles of barren coastline charted, but no encouraging reports about a Northwest Passage. In effect, he had wasted another expedition and more than two years in the vain quest of a Strait of Anian.

One of his secondary missions had been to look for a party headed by John Franklin, a veteran of the effort to push across the Pole in 1818. In 1819 Franklin had led a survey party to Hearne's country at the mouth of the Coppermine River and had explored the coastline eastward—in river boats, scarcely more than canoes! The Franklin party mapped 550 miles of the northern limits of the continental landmass.

But they never met Parry, for Franklin did not reach Foxe Basin. He turned southward and tried to return to base, hundreds of miles away, by an overland midwinter trek. Suffering hideous hardships from cold and hunger, the party was almost wiped out. Of the 20 men who started, 10 died on the road, an Eskimo interpreter wandered off and was never seen again, and the 9 survivors had only a few days of life left in them when they reached safety.

Although Parry had been turned back by ice in Prince Regent Inlet on his first voyage, he stubbornly clung to the notion that the Northwest Passage was best sought close to the continental coastline in as southern a latitude as possible. So on his third effort, again with *Hecla* and *Fury*, he headed for the inlet, where ice drove the *Fury* hopelessly aground. Parry cached *Fury*'s supplies on the beach and sailed the *Hecla* for home, having accomplished almost nothing.

Franklin had returned to the scene of his earlier near-disaster and had supervised exploration of more of the continental northern coastline westward from the Coppermine River. Later expeditions by Hudson's Bay men finished the work, so that virtually the entire continental coast was mapped from Alaska to 4.5° east of the Coppermine River.

With all the coming and going in the Arctic, John Ross brooded at home over his loss of face and the galling success of the younger officers who came after him. He proposed new ventures, but finally realized that the implacably hostile admiralty had no intention of backing him in another venture. So he turned to private sources and persuaded Felix Booth, sheriff of the City of London and a wealthy distiller, to back another trip into the ice—this time with the dual mission of locating the North Magnetic Pole and of finding the Northwest Passage.

Ross bought the *Victory*, a small ship of 85 tons that was fitted with sails but also powered by steam and paddle wheels. Among the 22 members of his expedition, he included his nephew, Comdr. James Ross, who was making his fifth Arctic voyage and would later become one of the most important explorers at the South Pole. Young Ross had become an outstanding authority on the earth's magnetic fields.

With 1,000 days' provisions aboard, Ross sailed into Prince Regent Inlet and found the site where the *Fury* had been abandoned. The ship had been crushed and sunk, but its supplies were almost intact where Parry had cached them ashore. After helping himself to all he could carry, Ross pushed ahead as best he could with a leaky old steam engine.

On October 8, 1829, he dug in for winter in Felix Harbor on Boothia Peninsula, both named for his sponsor. Ross lightened ship and assuaged his irritation by ditching the crotchety old steam engine.

The *Victory* stayed icebound for two winters. Ross, a fanatical teetotaler, kept up the amenities by serving high tea daily at five o'clock. He also made close friendships among the neighboring Eskimos and endeared himself to one native, who had lost a leg in a hunting accident, by ordering the ship's carpenter to shape him a wooden leg.

Ross studied the Eskimo way of life intensively. He showed more competence as an Arctic leader than many explorers rated higher in some circles, by perceiving the clue to Arctic survival in the native way of life.

"It would be very desirable indeed if the men could acquire the taste for Greenland food; since all experience has shown that the large use of oil and fat meats is the true secret of life in these frozen countries, and that the natives cannot subsist without it; becoming diseased, and dying. . . ."

The younger Ross made his own observations during long sled trips over the ice with Eskimo companions in search of the North Magnetic Pole.

"In the reindeer, the matters found in the stomachs are considered a great delicacy; and however our own might revolt at a vegetable dish cooked in this manner, this forms a very useful and salutary ingredient among their gross animal diet, since it is scarcely possible for them to collect any eatable vegetables by their own exertions."

On June 1, 1831, Commander Ross stood at 70° 05′ 17″ north and 96° 46′ west, where his vertical magnetic needle stood on end indicating he was over the North Magnetic Pole. (The magnetic pole wanders and has crossed the Northwest Passage to a midwater spot 7° farther north.)

With one of their main objectives thus achieved, and the discovery of a Northwest Passage daily looking less likely down ice-choked Prince Regent Inlet, Ross turned his thoughts homeward.

They were unable to crack the *Victory* loose, however, and so they loaded sleds and returned to the *Fury* cache, where they spent still another dreary winter. In June 1832 Ross faced a near mutiny. Unlike Henry Hudson, who meekly consented to discuss his personal shortcomings with his crew and lost his life for it, Ross "ordered the party to proceed, in a manner not easily misunderstood, and by an argument too peremptory to be disputed." Historians agree that John Ross probably persuaded his crew to recognize his qualities of leadership with the help of a very large, loaded gun.

By August 1833 they saw enough clear water to make a dash for Baffin Bay in the ship's boats. At 4:00 A.M. on August 26, near the entrance to Lancaster Sound, the explorers sighted a sailing ship. (I was at the same spot at the same season and can testify that there was enough light for me to read my notebooks at 4:00 A.M., a feat I cannot always accomplish at high noon.)

When the ship's rescue boat approached within hailing distance, Ross asked its identity. The mate, in answering, could not help indulging in a bit of name-dropping.

"The *Isabella* of Hull—once commanded by Captain Ross."

"I am Captain Ross."

But the mate was not to be gulled by every Tom, Dick, and Harry he bumped into in Lancaster Sound, so he assured Ross that he had been dead for at least two years.

Once convinced of Ross's identity, the mate raced back to the ship and the crew manned the rigging, cheering in wild excitement at seeing fellow seamen return from the dead. And small wonder that the explorers had been abandoned as lost, for they had spent three winters locked in the ice and out of touch with the world.

But far from perishing with all his men, Ross had brought out all but three of his followers alive and whole, an extraordinary achievement.

King William IV knighted John Ross. Parliament voted a £5,000 reward and repaid Felix Booth the £18,000 he had spent on the trip. Although the navy had no obligation for the trip, it paid the crew double wages for the time till the *Victory* had been abandoned and full time from then. Commander Ross became a captain.

But most important to Sir John was vindication of his career and reestablishment as one of the giants of ice navigation.

The admiralty gathered itself for one more assault on the Northwest Passage, this time going all out to guarantee success.

Newly returned from a voyage into the ice near the South Pole under command of Capt. James Ross, the ships *Erebus* and *Terror* were prepared for another venture into the ice. Already strengthened for the southern trip, the two ships were further reinforced, given 50-horsepower auxiliary steam engines —though the bunkers carried only a ten-day supply of coal— and fitted with a newly invented screw propeller. Provisioners carried aboard supplies for three years, porcelain china, crystal glass and silver table settings for the messrooms, a 1,200-volume library, and a barrel organ with 50 selections.

But the 130 officers and men of the expedition wore only regulation blue uniforms, more suitable for the climate of the waters about the British Isles than for the Canadian Arctic.

Despite Sir John Ross's discovery that explorers venturing into the Arctic did well to study Eskimo adaptations to the climate, the British navy appears to have learned little. Possibly the antagonism of the highest sea lords to Ross, because of his failure to transit Lancaster Sound on his first expedition, had prejudiced them against any recommendation he might make.

In any case, the John Franklin expedition sailed from home in May 1845 with the confident expectation of the entire kingdom that the Northwest Passage was finally to be conquered.

Off Greenland, a whaling ship sighted the ships headed for Lancaster Sound. The *Erebus* and *Terror* sailed out of sight of the whalers—and of all mankind for all time.

By 1847 the Royal Navy began to worry about the silence and initiated relief expeditions to comb the Arctic archipelago from east, west, and south. The first to sail, under Sir James Ross, left in May 1848. No less than 40 expeditions followed in the next nine years—government and private, by sea and land, English and American—in the greatest show of concern for fellow human beings in the entire nineteenth century.

As a by-product of the rescue effort, searchers mapped immense stretches of the Canadian and Alaskan Arctic.

In 1850 Robert M'Clure sailed in the *Investigator* around Cape Horn, up the Pacific, through Bering Strait, across the Beaufort Sea, and into Prince of Wales Strait. He was stopped by ice; nevertheless, he pushed on by sled and climbed a hill from where he sighted the distant shore of Melville Island, the farthest point of land reached by Parry in 1819.

In effect, the Northwest Passage had been explored from end to end, for one Englishman had seen the sea-lanes leading from the east and another had just overlapped his vision from the west. And all was water from end to end.

Or rather ice.

For M'Clure had to turn back, thwarted from being the first man to sail the length of the passage by the finger of polar ice that probes part way down Prince of Wales Strait. He sailed around Banks Island and tried to reach the same goal by M'Clure Strait. But the truly formidable pack rammed into M'Clure Strait, trapped the *Investigator* in a harbor on the north shore of Banks Island, and forced M'Clure to spend two years trying to break out.

The waters of the eastern reaches of the Northwest Passage were teeming with search vessels and sled parties. The population of the Canadian Arctic archipelago was, during the period of the search for Franklin, almost as large as today. While preparing to dig a grave for a sailor who had just died, M'Clure saw a figure approaching across the ice from the east.

"From his pace and gestures we . . . naturally supposed at first that he was some one of our party pursued by a bear, but as we approached him doubts arose as to who it could be. He was certainly unlike any of our men; but recollecting that it was possible some one might be trying a new travelling dress, preparatory to the departure of our sledges, and certain that no one else was near, we continued to advance. When within about two hundred yards of us, this strange figure threw up his arms, and made gesticulations resembling those used by Esquimaux, besides shouting, at the top of his voice, words which, from the wind and the intense excitement of the moment, sounded like a wild screech; and this brought us both fairly to a stand-still. The stranger came quietly on, . . . , and really at that moment we might be pardoned for wondering whether he was a denizen of this or the other world, and had he but given us a glimpse of a tail or a cloven hoof, we should assuredly have taken to our legs: as it was, we gallantly stood our ground, and had the skies fallen upon us, we could hardly have been more astonished than when the . . . stranger called out,—

'I'm Lieutenant Pim, late of the *Herald*, and now in the *Resolute*. Captain Kellett is in her at Dealy Island!' "

M'Clure and his men traveled across the ice to the *Resolute*. In a fiasco of indecision and incompetence, the commander in chief of all search vessels, a Sir Edward Belcher, abandoned five ships and crammed all hands aboard the *North Star*. With the providential arrival of two supply ships, the survivors were divided to relieve crowding.

The flotilla arrived in England September 28, 1854, and M'Clure was hailed as the first man to transit the entire Northwest Passage, though indeed he did it in three ships and by sledge.

Virtually no historians have noted that a Lt. Gurney Cresswell and a few sailors, including a demented man of the *Investigator's* crew, had returned aboard the *Phoenix* a year earlier and were the true heroes. And at this late date, it is hopeless to correct history. So Cresswell must remain unsung.

Courts-martial cleared both M'Clure and Belcher for abandoning their ships. M'Clure was knighted, but Belcher never recovered reputation.

One of the abandoned ships, the *Resolute* of Capt. Henry Kellett, drifted with the ice 1,000 miles into Baffin Bay and Davis Strait. American whalers found the ship almost exactly a year after Belcher abandoned it, and brought it to Connecticut where the U.S. government bought it, refurbished it, and presented it as a gift to Queen Victoria.

Bits and fragments from the Franklin expedition have been turning up ever since, the latest being several depots of supplies found by Canadian airmen in 1952. Historians have reconstructed the fate of the lost expedition by working from clues buried in Eskimo legends, bodies, and pieces of equipment found scattered about the Arctic and the astonishingly skimpy written records left by Franklin's officers.

After attempting and abandoning a probe northward through Wellington Channel, Franklin wintered on Beechey Island. Headstones mark the graves of three of his sailors who died there. He probably left Beechey Island in August—perhaps hastily, for he left behind a litter of useful material. He forced his way southward down Peel Sound and froze in for a second winter at about 70° north 90° west. The men were still in good enough condition to spend the winter on sled explorations of the neighborhood and on May 28, 1847, a Lt. Graham Gore was able to leave a message at Cape Felix with the cheery note, "All's well."

But a year later, on April 25, 1848, Comdr. James Fitzjames, executive officer to the expedition, wrote on the margins of

Gore's note that Franklin had died on June 11, 1847, and that 9 other officers, including the Lieutenant Gore who had written the original message, had died, as had 15 men. The 105 survivors had crossed the ice to King William Island.

Commander Fitzjames added that the survivors were starting the next day for Back's Fish River—a desperate enterprise indeed, for the nearest help in that direction, a Hudson's Bay post, lay almost a thousand miles across some of the world's most hostile country, the great Barren Lands of northern Canada. The choice of that grim road to rescue is all the more puzzling since the immense stocks from Parry's *Fury*, that had once served Sir John Ross well, still lay on a beach only 250 miles northeast.

With incredible stupidity, the weakened survivors dragged behind them 1,400-pound boats on sledges loaded with the most astounding trash, like elaborate silver table service. Men dropped beside the trail and lay unburied where they died. Some explorers who later found bodies with arms and legs sawn off believe that some of the survivors resorted to cannibalism. About 40 men dragged themselves as far as the Canadian mainland and died there near the shore, probably in the winter of 1848–49.

With the discovery that the Northwest Passage was choked with ice too thick for merchant ships of the day, interest died. The rest of the history of the Northwest Passage, to recent times, is anticlimactic, largely because the competence of the explorers involved prevented the kind of misadventures that make good reading. Franklin was the last of the bumbleheads who made exciting stories by supervising disasters in the Northwest Passage.

In 1903 a young Norwegian named Roald Amundsen sailed the 47-ton herring boat *Gjøa* into Lancaster Sound, bound for Bering Strait like hundreds of mariners before him. But this young mariner was in no hurry, for he wished to make leisurely observations of the earth's magnetism along the way. He spent two winters at Gjøa Haven on the south shore of King William Island, prospering and making voluminous notes in the same landscape where Franklin's men had perished. Amundsen and his crew made long sled journeys filling in blanks on Arctic maps, and they reported that the site of Franklin's disaster was an Arctic paradise teeming with fish and game.

On August 13, 1905, the ice cracked and the *Gjøa* sailed off, hugging the northern shore of the continent. On August 27 Amundsen awakened to the cry, "Vessel in sight, sir!"

The ship was a whaler from the Pacific, which meant that the *Gjøa* had become the first vessel to transit the Northwest Passage.

The *Gjøa* froze in for a third winter near Herschel Island, on the Canada-Alaska frontier. The situation was positively cozy, for 11 whalers had frozen in nearby. Their sailors, Eskimos, and the crewmen of the *Gjøa* had a fine social season. One of Amundsen's sailors died after a short illness and an Eskimo cabin boy later drowned.

On August 31, 1906, the *Gjøa* received a boisterous welcome in Nome, Alaska, a port on the far side of Bering Strait. After 400 years a vessel had gone from Atlantic to Pacific over the top of North America.

Amundsen's reports of the thickness of ice and difficulties of navigation cooled the ardor of possible explorers, especially since the deed had now been done.

In 1944 the Royal Canadian Mounted Police schooner *St. Roch*, under command of Sgt. Henry Larsen, crossed from west to east in a two-year journey. In 1944 Sergeant Larsen and *St. Roch* crossed from east to west in one season on a route followed precisely by the S.S. *Manhattan* 25 years later.

H.M.C.S. *Labrador*, commanded by Capt. O. C. S. Robertson,

followed the same route in 1954 in the first transit by a deep draft vessel.

In 1956 three U.S. Coast Guard ships, *Storis*, *Spar*, and *Bramble*, made the passage by a different route. Those first U.S. ships to make the passage were led through the treacherous Bellot Strait by *Labrador*, this time under command of Capt. Tom C. Pullen.

The world of ice navigation is a small one. During the *Manhattan* cruise, *Storis* was badly damaged by ice in Alaskan waters; Capt. Tom Pullen, now retired from the Canadian navy, was Canadian liaison officer aboard the *Manhattan*.

The nuclear submarines *Nautilus*, *Skate*, and *Seadragon* in 1958 crossed the top of the world, but their voyages far below the ice were so uneventful that they might have been cruising off Key Biscayne.

And so the great adventure seemed to run down from lack of incentive, till the day in 1968 when drillers from a combined Humble-Atlantic Richfield team tapped incentive aplenty, by proving a vast underground oil field that already ranks as by far the largest in North America and eventually may prove largest in the world.

89

In an unprecedented move to speed conversion of the S.S. Manhattan *from tanker to armored icebreaker, Sun Shipyard and Dry Dock Company of Chester, Pa., cut the ship into four pieces, put the conventional bow into storage, sent one midship section to Newport News, Va., and another to Mobile, Ala., ordered an armored prow of revolutionary design from Bath, Me., and built a new armored forward section to further protect the main hull. More than 3,000 workmen swarmed over the stern section in Chester, beefing up internal struts and fitting at the waterline a 14-foot-high blister made of 2-inch steel to protect the vulnerable, thin-skinned hull. Riveters and chippers made the days hideous with their clamor. At night the guttering blue light of welder's arcs lit the sky over the Delaware River.*

To equip the Manhattan *for battling ice, workers replaced conventional screws with specially blended bronze-nickel alloy propellers of 28-foot diameter. They chewed up blocks of granite-hard ice as big as bungalows and came through the voyage without blemish.*

In dawn hours, the night crew pulled together the armored prow from Maine and the Sun-built bow section.

After weeks of delay, S.S. Manhattan *sails under Delaware Memorial Bridge bound for sea trials.*

In 1497 the Genoese John Cabot, sailing for the merchant adventurers of Bristol, made a first assault on the icy route across the top of North America. His minuscule craft, the Mathew, *weighed about one-twenty-fifth the mass of the* Manhattan's *conventional bow, cut off and left in storage at Chester. Cabot discovered Nova Scotia and possibly Newfoundland but failed to penetrate northern ice.*

Undaunted by the history of disaster befalling previous expeditions, on August 24, 1969, the Manhattan *stood down Delaware River bound for the Arctic graveyard of hundreds of brave ships and men.*

Out of ballast, the armored prow shows the sharklike profile meant to crush polar ice under the ponderous weight of the great ship pushed by 43,000 horsepower.

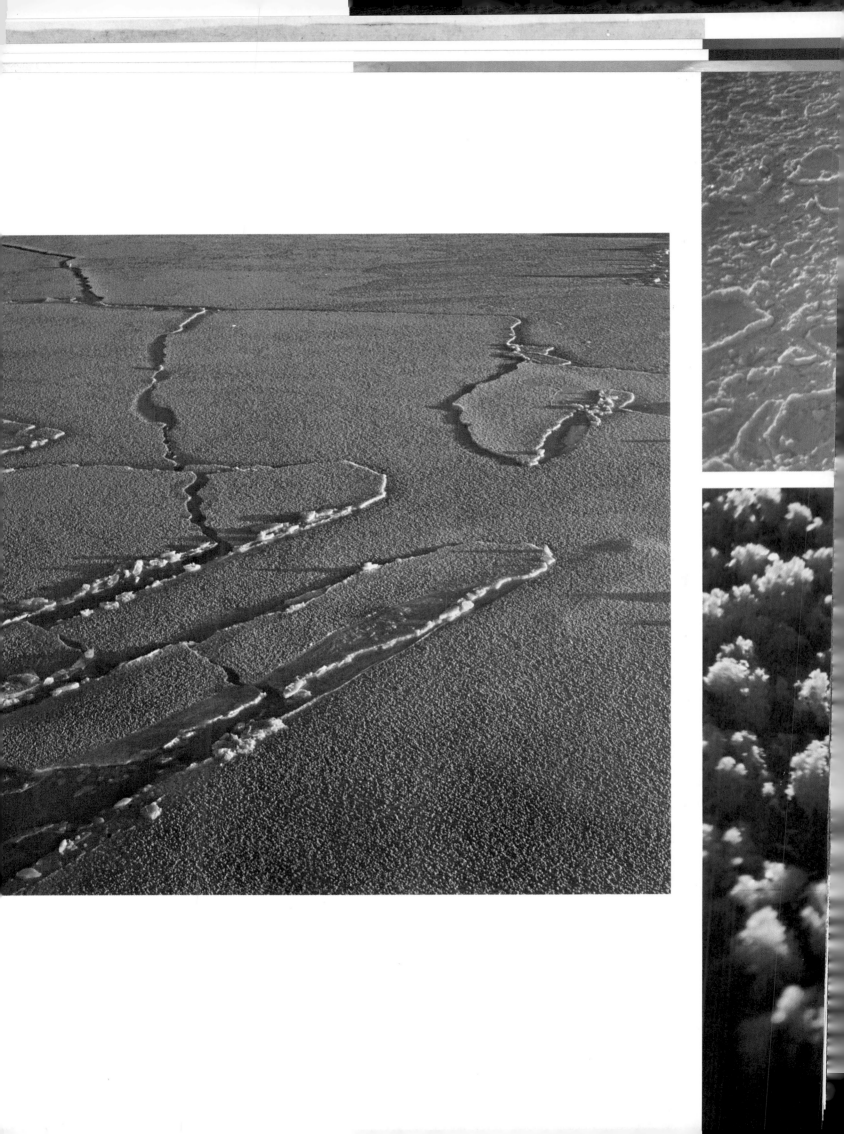

Pushed by the wind, solid ice sheets crack and slide over each other in the curious pattern called finger rafting (opposite page).

Sometimes wind turbulence grinds cakes together into circular pancakes rimmed with a lip of crystals.

During the night, sharp frosts deposit the scanty water vapor of the Arctic in the incredibly delicate crystals called ice flowers.

During the brief summers, ice melts on the surface of the pack, but melting rarely reaches through to seawater below the floe. Early in the winter, melt pools refreeze in a glassy surface contrasting with the weathered hummocks of the old pack. The friendly-looking melt pools deceive, for the salt has leached from them and they have refrozen as freshwater ice, considerably more dangerous than the grimmer-looking rough ice about them.

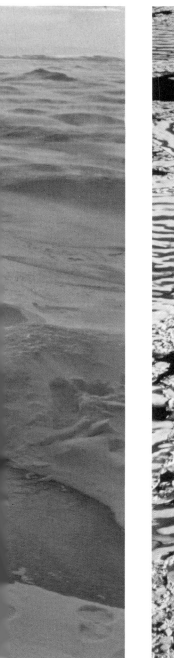

With 80 percent of the world's population and 90 percent of its industry between 35° and 50° north, the moguls of trade and foreign policy do well to study the globe from a view over the North Pole to see the true relation between the centers of power and commerce.

The Manhattan's route through the Northwest Passage is the only one that is possible for deep-draft vessels—except for a detour through M'Clure Strait, a route choked by possibly the most dangerous ice pack in the Northern Hemisphere.

Alarmed by mounting threats to the world's environment, Canadians and Americans have demanded reassurance that the fragile Arctic ecology will not be damaged by the oil boom.

A major oil spill into Arctic waters would be an unimaginable disaster, and oil company officials, painfully sensitive about the issue, plan elaborate safeguards. Many conservationists are demanding that future ships have self-contained sewage and garbage systems to avoid contaminating the Far North.

Ice provides its own insulation and will rarely freeze more than about nine feet thick, no matter how low the temperature. Storms drive floes before the winds, however, and tremendous forces push the ice into pressure ridges many feet thicker than the normal pack. Nuclear submarines have reported downthrusting ridges hundreds of feet deep.

The waters of M'Clure Strait north of Banks Island suffer terrible storms from the Arctic Ocean to the west, piling the polar ice trapped in the strait into a 220-mile-long plug of dangerous ridges.

Icebreaking experts, trained in the grim fields of the Baltic, the route above Siberia, the Antarctic, gaped in astonishment when the Manhattan *bored into fields of polar ice, cracking floes occasionally 20 feet thick and upending chunks as big as a bungalow. The clamor immediately over the cutwater was deafening, but amidships only the wind whistling in the rigging disturbed the Arctic silence.*

The revolutionary clipper-ship prow behaved beautifully, shooting a long crack forward, often for miles, thus providing a safety valve, a place where the ice displaced by our passage could go.

Contrary to a widespread misconception, an ice-breaker in thick ice does not open a clear channel once and for all. Only yards behind the Manhattan the broken ice has closed in. Huge chunks, turned on edge by the ship's passage, have re-frozen into a nightmare jumble. Among ice navigators an old chestnut goes: "An icebreaker is an ice-maker."

On the horizon the Manhattan's Canadian and American escort icebreakers stand ready to help Big Brother break free.

In 1819 in an extraordinary exploit, Lt. William Edward Parry of the Royal Navy sailed two wooden-hulled ships powered only by canvas to the middle of the redoubtable M'Clure Strait before being stopped by the ice. It was 150 years before the armored Manhattan, driven by 43,000 horses and guided by American and Canadian scouts in helicopters and airplanes, could penetrate nearly so far into M'Clure Strait. Seeking shelter for the winter, Parry's men cut their way through new ice into Winter Harbour on Melville Island. To amuse themselves, they rigged sails on the ice chunks and sailed them out to sea.

When crew members visited the Franklin cairn on Beechey Island, the "post office of the Arctic," they left a letter memorializing a venture in northern exploration unequaled in international cooperation. Scuba divers from the U.S. Coast Guard icebreaker Staten Island *braved icy waters to inspect the hull for damage. Ice scientists from the army's Cold Regions Research and Engineering Laboratory, the University of Alaska, Scott Polar Institute, the Canadian and American governments gathered data on ice formations in regions never before visited by man.*

Working in an infant science, cold-regions experts improvised hand tools to probe floes. Almost any information gathered, even the simple temperature of water, made a valued contribution to the meager store of scientific knowledge about the Arctic seas.

The landscape of the Arctic is dreary and forbidding, as at Prudhoe Bay, but heavenly bodies gleam through the clean cold air with a beauty unrivaled elsewhere in the world.

Nevertheless, all hands thrilled to the murky beauty of the New York skyline (overleaf) as the battered Manhattan *steamed ponderously up New York Narrows to a berth where families and friends prepared a welcome home.*

Chapter 5

THE VOYAGE
OF S.S. *MANHATTAN*

Sea Goddess Feeding Young by Saggiassie

Birds Walking by Sharni

Groping with felt-lined boot, I touched the frozen surface below the ladder and stepped off the craft to a virgin wilderness of bone-gnawing cold—the first man ever to put his feet on that stretch of universe.

Just a few days before, uncounted millions of people all over the globe had halted business to watch Neil Armstrong's boot grope for the moon's untrodden surface. But nobody stopped his work to watch my historic descent. Although the icy surface of Viscount Melville Sound where I was standing had never supported a man any more than had Armstrong's lunar stamping ground, the comings and goings of fellow explorers in the S.S. *Manhattan's* flotilla had made a commonplace of venturing a foot onto virgin wilderness.

We did not become so blasé, however, that we ceased to wonder at the alien beauty of the unearthly scene. At 74° northern latitude, the sun in that early winter season spent hours in a flaming sunrise to a low angle above the noontime horizon and spent the rest of the rapidly shortening days setting in fiery skies. Blowing snow glowed with the orange and apricot tints of the eerie sky, and the shadow side of jumbled blocks of ice that were heaved up in pressure ridges showed the deep purple hue of the grape.

Sailors from Oil Patch in the southern United States, journalists at home in the climatized offices of Madison Avenue, and engineers from cozy drafting rooms in Houston found that expanse of wind-driven ice more alien than Armstrong's moon.

But the reason for their improbable presence in that hostile waste between the barren hills of Melville Island and the grim escarpment of Stefansson Island, they found not strange at all.

In 1968, discovery at Prudhoe Bay on Alaska's North Slope of a vast underground reservoir of oil—some sources estimate at least 25 billion barrels—had lured throngs of drilling teams into the tundra where once only the migrating caribou and the occasional Eskimo ever strayed. At sea, we Arctic explorers, looking for a cheap water route from the Alaskan oil fields to the oil-thirsty market on the East Coast of the United States, were startling polar bears and white foxes that till then had ruled the frozen waterways undisturbed by man.

In possibly the largest gamble of any commercial enterprise in history, Humble Oil & Refining Company, domestic subsidiary of the Standard Oil Company of New Jersey, had bet $36 million on this single exploratory trip of the tanker S.S. *Manhattan*. British Petroleum and Atlantic Richfield each chipped in another $2 million. Largest commercial ship flying the American flag, the 150,000-ton *Manhattan* had been rebuilt as an icebreaker-oceanographic research vessel to test the feasibility of transporting Alaska's North Slope oil by the Northwest Passage.

I joined the ship's company on a blistering August day in a Chester, Pennsylvania, shipyard. Resting after a six-story climb up a ladder to the deck of the S.S. *Manhattan*, I studied the vast stretch of steel that would be my playground for two months. The 1,005 feet of deck, as long as three football fields and almost as wide, sprawled over three acres. Displacing more than 11 times as much as the U.S.S.R.'s *Moscow*, the *Manhattan's* 150,000 tons made it the largest icebreaker afloat. (Armored blisters eight feet wide, fixed along the waterline to protect the thin-skinned inner hull from steel-hard polar ice, gave the ship the hulking shoulders of a professional fullback.

The specially designed ice-cutting prow looked more like the bowsprit of a Yankee clipper than an honest steamship.)

Immediately after being tapped for the voyage, the volunteer crews and scientists had pored over the books of previous explorations with fascination, marveling at the courage and persistence of those who had gone before us. But the very perils that had gained fame for those earlier mariners had till recent months denied hope of profitable commercial use of the Northwest Passage. Impressed by the tons of high-tensile steel and the immense propellers driven by 43,000-horsepower turbines, half of the observers had total confidence we would broach a bottle of champagne in Alaska within three weeks. The other half— admittedly containing virtually all the ice-experienced navigators—remained skeptical.

And so, on August 24, 1969, many of the scientists and observers among the 126 persons aboard the *Manhattan* sailed down the Delaware River, headed for the Arctic with a sense of foreboding only partly relieved by whistle salutes of passing tankers, cheers of crowds along the riverbanks, and the roar of a flotilla of pleasure craft and light planes escorting us to sea.

Nerves grew more taut during the night of September 1, 1969, off the west coast of Greenland, when the first little growlers, vanguard of the grim iceberg fleet awaiting us farther north in Baffin Bay, clunked and jangled along the armored blister protecting the thin-skinned inner hull. That same night our Canadian icebreaker escort, the *John A. Macdonald*, joined us only seconds off from the appointed time and yards off the place of rendezvous set weeks before. Such seamanlike precision soothed troubled spirits by auguring well for the weeks of work together lying ahead.

Next day we sighted a vast field of ice along the shores of Baffin Island to the west—the notorious Baffin pack that crushed and sank half a thousand whaling ships during the nineteenth century. Although open water lay all about, Capt. Roger Steward, the ship's master, was eager to give his ship its baptism of ice, and he turned the armored cutwater west. The ship nosed among its first floes.

Waves lapped noisily against the ice as we silently glided nearer, undercutting the surface and leaving tabletops supported on slender stems. But those tabletops projected high from the water, betraying subsurface blocks 12 and 14 feet thick.

Rails crowded by all off-watch hands, the ship pushed its cutwater against the first floe, broke off a half-acre chunk, tilted it with roaring cascades of green water, and sailed ponderously by without a quiver.

Picking up confidence, the ship's officers called for more speed. Gigantic floes cracked, heaved, spun out of our road, roared, and plunged as they shattered into fragments. Elated by success, officers called for ten knots and bore down on a massive block a square mile in area and, judging from the projecting ridges, possibly 60 feet thick in parts.

Experienced officers among the liaison parties aboard, from American and Canadian icebreaker services, blanched as they understood the conning officer's intent.

"They're going to smash their toy first day out of the wrappings," said one of the veterans of the ice-breaking service off both coasts of Greenland.

Hands gripped railings to resist the shock of impact with the mighty floe.

The cutwater bit into the floe. Feeling the immense weight of the *Manhattan*, driven by 43,000 horses, the floe cracked with sharp popping sounds, and pieces of ice as big as harbor seals soared in wide arcs to the side. Cracks ran outward and forward from the *Manhattan*'s armored prow and chunks of ice as big as boxcars split off, rolled their cobalt-blue edges to the sky, and scraped down the armored blister with agonizing shrieks. Under the stupendous pressure generated by the impact, plumes of salt spray shot 60 feet high and drenched the scientists hanging over the rail to get a better view of the action.

And the deck of the great ship remained as rock-steady underfoot as the icy mountains dimly visible on the horizon.

The experienced officers, so recently horrified by the reckless attack on that dangerous block, looked at each other with mouths agape.

Martti Saarikangas, of Finland's major icebreaker shipyard and veteran of many passages through the Northeast Passage across Siberia, leaned over the bridge rail to watch the cobalt-blue face of the newly shattered floe grind by.

"This ship just broke more ice than any ship in history and that includes the famous Russians," he said to me, "even the mighty *Moscow*.

"But before you start planning parties in Alaska, remember an isolated floe, even one so huge as the one we just broke, gives only child's-play resistance compared to a continuous pack under heavy wind pressure like the ones in the western reaches of the Canadian archipelago."

Ominous noises from the engine room gang further checked runaway enthusiasm.

Many of those enormous chunks of the broken floe had passed the length of the flat underside of the ship and emerged in the screws. The uproar as the ice kablunked along the bottom like a procession of cyclopean square wheels, and the hideous uproar below decks as the propellers battered the chunks heaving up from below, had almost chased the engine watch up the ladders for safety.

"When that ice hits the props, I feel like a squirrel trapped in a concrete mixer," Third Engineer Al Burns told me.

So we toned down the exuberance of our first victory and

proceeded soberly to Thule in Greenland where U.S.C.G.S. *Northwind*, our American icebreaker escort, awaited us.

First order of business was to call on the scuba-diving team from the *Johnny Mac* to plunge under the ice-flecked waters for an inspection of the screws.

The most skeptical observers felt a grudging and growing admiration for the ship when divers reported that even paint marks left on propeller blades by shipyard workers had come undisturbed through the terrible ice battering.

Reassured about the iceworthiness of his ship, Captain Steward crossed northern Baffin Bay, the North Water that is strangely and perpetually ice-free and that once swarmed with a vast fleet of whalers.

Skeins of geese passed overhead and gams of whales and porpoises crossed our path. Ice lookouts noticed that the animals were all headed south and wondered if they were trying to tell us something.

The *Manhattan* entered Lancaster Sound, eastern end of the pass through the Canadian archipelago. As we neared the magnetic pole off Bathurst Island, just yards off our course, our compasses went wild, the cards searching for north in spasmodic jerks across 100° of arc. Though the gyroscopic compasses had been specially adapted for far northern operation, the navigator Al Scara had to keep them honest through frequent celestial sights.

On the sun's surface, a storm 30 times wider than the earth's diameter spewed out charged particles that were bombarding the upper atmosphere over the magnetic pole, pushing it miles from its usual position. Even the *Manhattan's* powerful radios, 500 times stronger than most merchant installations, faded under the solar storm's buffeting. The communications blackout made me feel ominously isolated from the familiar world. I was crossing a desert where even the friendly sun, source of all life, had turned hostile. At night great curtains of northern lights, coiling and heaving under the bombardment of charged particles from the sun, signaled that we had chosen the peak of an 11-year sunspot cycle for our journey across the earth's magnetic vortex.

Most of Lancaster Sound had enough open water for easy navigation, but ice reconnaissance planes reported that a dangerous ice stream had blown down from the Pole through Byam Martin Channel and across our path through Viscount Melville Sound. A Canadian officer, visiting from the *Johnny Mac*, told me that his ship had rescued crews from two oil-exploration barges crushed and sunk in the ice ahead less than a month before.

That we did not yet rule the Arctic seas was underlined minutes later when we passed a polar bear feeding on a seal. Our immense size in that desolate landscape left the bear so unimpressed that he scarcely looked up from his meal to note our passage. The little Arctic fox that follows most bears to feast on their leftovers never took his eye from the half-eaten seal.

On the bridge I idled away time by watching a gam of perhaps a hundred beluga whales feeding along the bleak shores of Byam Martin Island. Capt. Tom Pullen, liaison officer for the Canadian ice services and possibly the most experienced ice officer still active in the non-Communist world, kept his attention on the ship's course; he peered intently forward through binoculars.

"See the shafts of light running from the horizon to the underside of the clouds? That's 'ice blink' and it means the edge of the polar ice stream lies just below."

We got some hint of the interest in our voyage when a jet plane broke through the low overcast, and circled the *Manhattan* to give its passengers a closeup view. More than 100 passengers had paid $370 each to fly the 2,100 miles from Montreal, just for that two-minute look at our progress through the Northwest Passage.

And that progress soon came to a halt after we had bashed our way deep into the polar ice stream. For the ship lost way and stopped in a tangle of weathered pressure ridges, broken and uptilted by storm winds, leached of salt in summer melts, and refrozen into cobalt-blue freshwater ice hard enough to cut through ordinary steel plating like a cold chisel through a tin can.

To make some profit from the mishap, the skipper unleashed the ice scientists who had been clamoring for a chance to practice their strange craft. They swarmed down ladders and scattered about the floe to set up open-air workshops. With hand-twisted bits and core samplers they measured ice thickness, strength, and salinity. Each party carried a 30.06 rifle in case a bear challenged their right to invade his northern seas.

Before descending to the ice, I armed myself with a survival luncheon of smoked salmon and cream cheese for appetizer, Rock Cornish game hen for main course, honeydew melon for dessert, and English beer for beverage. (The *Manhattan's* crew faced little danger of starving or languishing from scurvy, for Chief Steward Leo Oliveira had jammed the larder with supplies for six months, including 8,000 quarts of milk, 4,200 dozen large eggs, 2,500 steaks of various choice cuts, 764 turkeys, 789 ducks, 424 chickens, and 360 of the little game birds I selected for my survival kit.)

Off-duty sailors from all the ships in our little flotilla mingled on the ice. In that one square mile or so in mid-channel of Viscount Melville Sound, our 500 head count came to almost double the population of the entire 168,000-square-mile Queen Elizabeth archipelago to the north of us. Like sailors everywhere, they began a brisk commerce, swapping cigars, color film, gloves, tobacco, cigarette lighters, snapshots, and headgear. (For the rest of the voyage the sailors of the *Manhattan* wore the jaunty beret of the Canadian icebreaker service, bought with the riches of our overflowing slop chest.)

A cold wind from the Pole sprang up. I took off my down ski mittens to change film in a camera. The cold struck savagely, and almost instantly I lost muscular suppleness in my fingers. But I did not lose feeling, for my fingers felt as though the nails were aflame and burning off the ends. The film turned brittle and cracked. A job that ordinarily takes 30 seconds cost me three minutes of sharp discomfort.

Around the horizon mirages loomed. Two and three coastlines stacked up like layers of a wedding cake. They melted away as I watched, and a field of broken ice shapes, looking like the fantasy skyline of a city of the future, loomed in their place. In that shimmering shifting light I enlisted among the sympathizers of Sir John Ross, who suffered a blasted career for sighting nonexistent mountains that seemed to close off Lancaster Sound.

When I started back for the ship, some new trick of the light wiped out all shadows and with them the dimension of depth. I had to grope for each step, not knowing exactly where the foothold was. Just short of the ship's ladder I missed my footing, crashed heavily to the ice, and badly wrenched a shoulder by trying to protect my cameras. Aboard the ship, Dr. Charles Swithinbank, a British glaciologist, had witnessed my fall and assured me that I was not the first explorer to suffer from the trickeries of polar light.

"On an earlier expedition," he said, "a party of my friends pulling a loaded sled across what they thought a level ice field stepped off a sixty-foot cliff, bashing out their teeth and breaking bones at a frightful rate."

After gathering in the ice parties, the captain prepared to hurl the ship against the ice again. But he discovered that we were locked in more firmly than before. Contrary to widespread belief, an icebreaker does not break a channel that stays open for an entire season—or even for an entire hour. As the popular saying among ice navigators has it, "An icebreaker is an ice-maker."

When an icebreaker bashes a cake of ice into jumbled brash, pressure from the pack on both sides presses the channel closed almost immediately, forcing the brash down deeper than the original cake. So when it refreezes, which it does almost instantly, the wake of an icebreaker is a solid plug of ice considerably deeper than it was before the ship's passage.

Trying to back into our refrozen wake to get room for a new ramming charge, we confirmed the *Manhattan's* inability to put more than one-third power into backing down—which is characteristic of all turbine-driven ships. So Captain Pullen called to the *Johnny Mac* for assistance:

"Would you mind coming over to nibble about our quarters."

And the *Johnny Mac* came gamboling through the ice as effortlessly as a frolicking puppy bounding through a flower bed. Capt. Paul Fournier of the *Johnny Mac* is a fiery French Canadian from the Gaspé Peninsula who has spent most of his life breaking ice. Because the potbellied shape of the *Johnny Mac* gave less resistance to the wind-driven ice than the *Manhattan's* long flat sides, Captain Fournier easily crunched into the ice around our port quarter in a dazzling show of seamanship that had all our ship's officers on the bridge as admiring spectators.

Crushing ice under his crimson prow till he lost way, Captain Fournier backed down for another charge and rammed ahead, passing within a hundred feet of our stern—a distance that fills warmwater sailors with horror.

The ice pressure on our stern loosened, we backed free and bulled on toward M'Clure Strait, the historic ice-choked channel that had turned back all previous assaults from the east.

And here our American icebreaker escort, *Northwind*, had to turn back and take the southern route, more or less the Amundsen route along the continental shelf. In those more sheltered channels, too shallow for the *Manhattan's* 57-foot draft, *Northwind* returned to Seattle to establish a historic first that passed virtually unnoticed. By coming from Seattle to Thule to meet us and returning to base, *Northwind* became the first vessel to make a Northwest Passage round trip in one season.

But failure of *Northwind*, a powerful icebreaker manned by professional ice navigators, to transit even Viscount Melville Sound (much less the more formidable M'Clure Strait) raises questions about the near deification of Lieutenant Parry, who almost made it through M'Clure in 1820. Without denigrating Parry's reputation as a mariner, I insist, as one who has been there, that his sail-powered wooden ships would not have reached within 200 miles of his farthest westing in 1819 had he encountered the ice we met in 1969. The tremendous role that luck plays in the building of reputations was proved by the mediocre performance of Parry's ships when he encountered truly formidable ice on his next two outings.

Prevailing westerly winds drive the polar ice of the Beaufort Sea into M'Clure Strait and jam it into a 220-mile-long ice plug of jumbled ridges as much as 20 feet high and 100 feet deep. No vessel has ever passed through that formidable barrier from east to west and we hoped to be the first, though we did stop repeatedly, temporarily defeated by the ice.

And then we struck a truly dangerous floe, a three-mile expanse of aged polar ice broken and refrozen into a nightmare tangle of ridges.

Conning officers backed and rammed for 12 hours trying to

crack loose. One officer during a single four-hour watch rang up 62 bells—orders for change of engine speed or direction—and one engineer set a record by spinning the control wheel from full ahead to full astern in 27 seconds. But we had been stuck before, and we still hoped.

But near midnight on September 11, 1969, Stanley Haas, the project director, roused out the press gang to report that M'Clure Strait had proved "beyond the capabilities of this test vessel.

"We are on a test voyage and our first duties are to the experiment. We would like to have been the first to make the Northwest Passage the hard way, of course, but we are not here to make history and must take the prudent course.

"So we shall turn back and take you on a scenic tour of Prince of Wales Strait and Amundsen Gulf where you'll see caribou and musk ox, seals and polar bear, all the exciting beauties of this Arctic land—except hopefully for more of this blamed polar ice."

Canadian planes flying scouting patrols ahead had taken a profile of the ice with laser beams and measured its age with infrared. A U.S. Coast Guard plane with experimental side-looking radar had mapped the ice in a ten-mile-wide path ahead. The films, dropped to us by parachute and picked up from the ice by helicopter for development aboard, showed 80 miles of worsening ice ahead.

So we turned back at 117° 30′ west, disgruntled by failure and only slightly mollified to learn that we had made the deepest penetration of the strait in history.

Shunning the polar floes we had once attacked eagerly, we slipped through leads our helicopters found for us. Using the helicopter reconnaissance and consulting the laser, infrared, and radar intelligence fed to us by supporting planes, we retraced in ten hours the route that had taken us four days going in.

In that first school of ice navigation for big ships ever conducted anywhere, our officers had to be teachers and pupils, making up lessons as they went along and learning them. The ice navigator's art is subtle, highly specialized, and almost impossible to communicate to an outsider. But in essence it consists of finding cracks in an apparently solid pack and avoiding head-on confrontation. As passengers on transpolar flights between Old and New World can testify, even at the North Pole the Arctic pack is not solid but riddled with flaws, called leads when they are long, narrow cracks, and polynias when they are large and round like ponds.

The *Manhattan's* officers learned their lessons well, for we never again called on the doughty little *Johnny Mac* during the westward voyage. (Later, scuba inspection showed that the *Johnny Mac* in its brave efforts to free us in M'Clure Strait had sheared off a blade of its starboard propeller.)

On September 14, 1969, our helicopter reconnaissance reported only ten miles of ice separated us from open water. Even in the short period of one trip through the ice, I had learned much of the Eskimo art of reading ice conditions ahead by reflections on the sky. A black streak on the clouds, the "water sky" that marks open sea, showed just before sunset.

So I stayed up that night to be present at the historic moment.

At 0234 the ship's prow broke the far edge of the polar ice and the ship swam free with only 1,000 miles of open sea between us and Barrow, Alaska, at the end of the road.

The *Manhattan* had made it, the first transit of the fabled Northwest Passage by a commercial vessel as forerunner of a fleet of icebreaker-tankers that might make use of Arctic waters a commonplace within less than a decade.

On our return, we found that in the advancing winter, channels that had been open on our outbound passage had frozen over. The days shortened rapidly; the lengthening darkness of the winter night settled over the waterways. Temperatures dropped to frighteningly low levels and gales' swept down from the north without warning. Despite our success in transiting the Arctic ice fields in both directions, we sailed the open Atlantic with a feeling of escape from a grim trap ready to spring closed on the unwary mariner at his first mistake.

And yet, so compelling is the lure of adventure to mankind, when the call goes out for seamen to man the ships that will brave that white desert, I know that hundreds of sailors will respond to the chance for finding fame and knowledge and riches in the icy passages across the top of the world.

BIBLIOGRAPHY

CAMERON, IÄN.   *Lodestone and Evening Star.* New York: E. P. Dutton & Co., Inc., 1966.

DODGE, ERNEST S.   *Northwest by Sea.* New York: Oxford University Press, 1961.

FREUCHEN, PETER.   *Book of the Eskimos.* Cleveland: The World Publishing Company, 1951.

FREUCHEN, PETER, and SALOMONSEN, FINN.   *The Arctic Year.* New York: G. P. Putnam's Sons, Inc., 1958.

HAKLUYT, RICHARD.   *The Portable Hakluyt's Voyages.* New York: The Viking Press, Inc., 1965.

LEDYARD, JOHN.   *John Ledyard's Journal of Captain Cook's Last Voyage.* Corvallis, Oreg.: Oregon State College, 1964.

McDONALD, LUCILE S.   *Search for the Northwest Passage.* Portland: Binfords & Mort, 1958.

MACKENZIE, ALEXANDER.   *Alexander Mackenzie's Voyage to the Pacific Ocean in 1793.* New York: Citadel Press, 1967.

MIERTSCHING, JOHANN.   *Frozen Ships.* New York: St. Martin's Press, Inc., 1967.

MOWAT, FARLEY, ed.   *Ordeal by Ice.* Boston: Little, Brown and Company, 1961.

NANSEN, FRIDTJOF.   *In Northern Mists.* London: Heinemann, 1911.

NEATBY, LESLIE H.   *In Quest of the Northwest Passage.* New York: Thomas Y. Crowell Company, 1962.

SPECK, GORDON.   *Samuel Hearne and the Northwest Passage.* Caldwell, Idaho: Caxton Printers, Ltd., 1963.

STEFANSSON, VILHJALMUR. *Northwest to Fortune*. New York: Duell, Sloan & Pearce, Inc., 1958.

Unsolved Mysteries of the Arctic. New York: P. F. Collier, Inc., 1962.

TYRRELL, JOSEPH B. *Documents Relating to the Early History of Hudson Bay*. Toronto: The Champlain Society, 1931.

VICTOR, PAUL EMILE. *Man and the Conquest of the Poles*. London: Hamish Hamilton, Ltd., 1964.

Geographical Discovery and Exploration in the Queen Elizabeth Islands. Geographical Branch, Mines and Technical Surveys, Memoir 3, Ottawa: The Queen's Printer, 1964.

North of 60 Prospectus. Ottawa: Department of Indian Affairs and Northern Development, 1969.

Pilot of Arctic Canada, Vol. 1. Ottawa: Canadian Hydrographic Surveys, 1965.

INDEX

About the author

Free-lance writer Bern Keating is the author
of three adult and seven young adult history
books. For 20 years he was a photographer
and his work appeared in many major
magazines. Born in Canada, he grew up in
the United States and graduated summa
cum laude from the University of Arkansas.
Later, he served as destroyer communications
officer in World War II. He is married and is
the father of a son and daughter. His home
is in Greenville, Mississippi.

and the photographer

Dan Guravich was born in Winnipeg,
Manitoba, and has been interested in
photography since his childhood. After
serving as an officer with the Calgary Tanks
in Europe in World War II, he received his
Ph.D. degree from the University of
Wisconsin and worked for several years as an
agricultural geneticist. Since then he has
been a free-lance magazine photographer.
He has two daughters and a
son. His home is also in Greenville,
Mississippi.

PRINTED IN THE U.S.A.